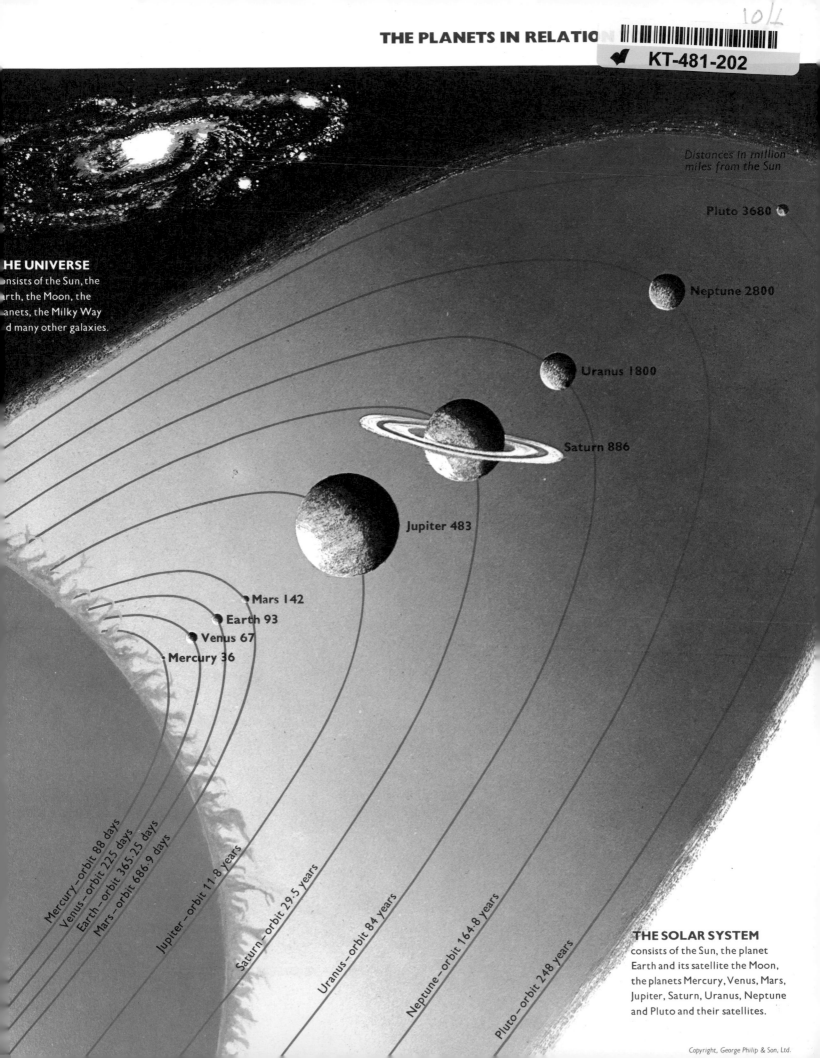

Distances in million miles from the Sun

Pluto 3680

Neptune 2800

Uranus 1800

Saturn 886

Jupiter 483

Mars 142

Earth 93

Venus 67

Mercury 36

THE UNIVERSE

...nsists of the Sun, the ...rth, the Moon, the ...anets, the Milky Way ...d many other galaxies.

Mercury – orbit 88 days
Venus – orbit 225 days
Earth – orbit 365·25 days
Mars – orbit 686·9 days
Jupiter – orbit 11·8 years
Saturn – orbit 29.5 years
Uranus – orbit 84 years
Neptune – orbit 164·8 years
Pluto – orbit 248 years

THE SOLAR SYSTEM

consists of the Sun, the planet Earth and its satellite the Moon, the planets Mercury, Venus, Mars, Jupiter, Saturn, Uranus, Neptune and Pluto and their satellites.

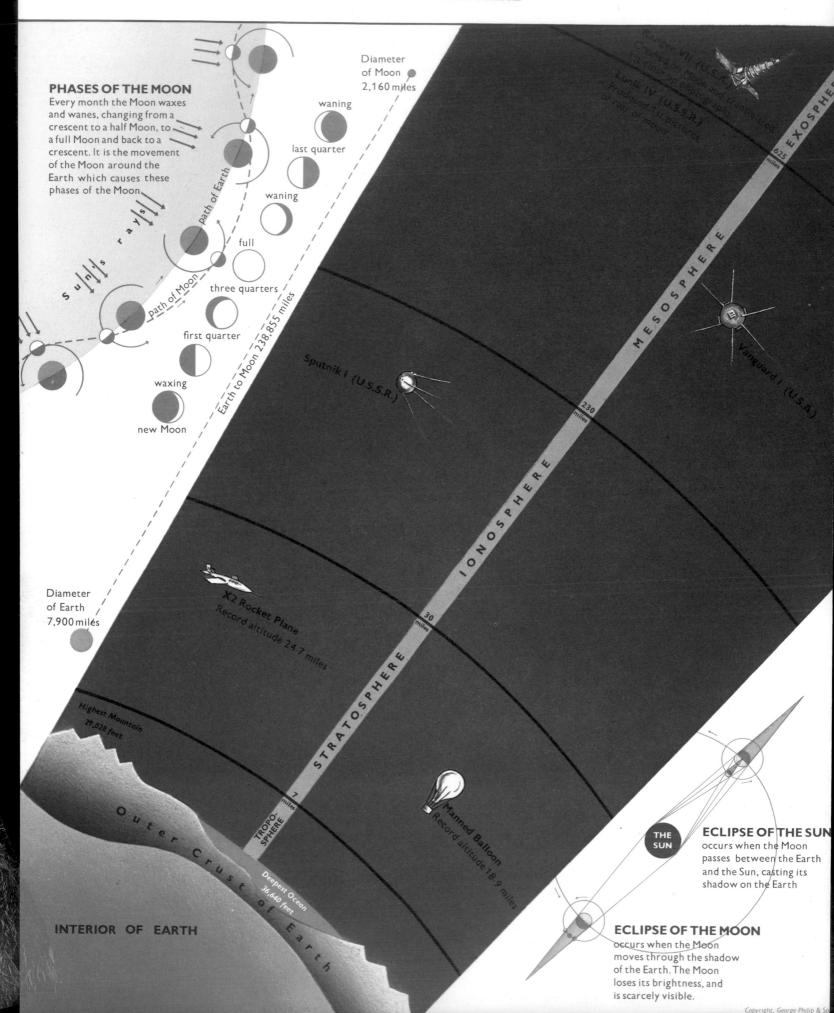

PHASES OF THE MOON

Every month the Moon waxes and wanes, changing from a crescent to a half Moon, to a full Moon and back to a crescent. It is the movement of the Moon around the Earth which causes these phases of the Moon.

Sun's rays

path of Earth

Path of Moon

waning

last quarter

waning

three quarters

full

first quarter

waxing

new Moon

Diameter of Moon 2,160 miles

Earth to Moon 238,855 miles

Diameter of Earth 7,900 miles

Ranger VII (U.S.A.) Crashed on Moon and transmitted 1st close-up photographs

Lunik IV (U.S.S.R.) Produced 1st pictures of rear of moon

EXOSPHERE

MESOSPHERE

625 miles

Vanguard I (U.S.A.)

IONOSPHERE

230 miles

Sputnik I (U.S.S.R.)

30 miles

STRATOSPHERE

X2 Rocket Plane
Record altitude 24.7 miles

7 miles

TROPO-SPHERE

Manned Balloon
Record altitude 18.9 miles

Highest Mountain
29,028 feet

Outer Crust of Earth

Deepest Ocean
36,640 feet

INTERIOR OF EARTH

THE SUN

ECLIPSE OF THE SUN

occurs when the Moon passes between the Earth and the Sun, casting its shadow on the Earth

ECLIPSE OF THE MOON

occurs when the Moon moves through the shadow of the Earth. The Moon loses its brightness, and is scarcely visible.

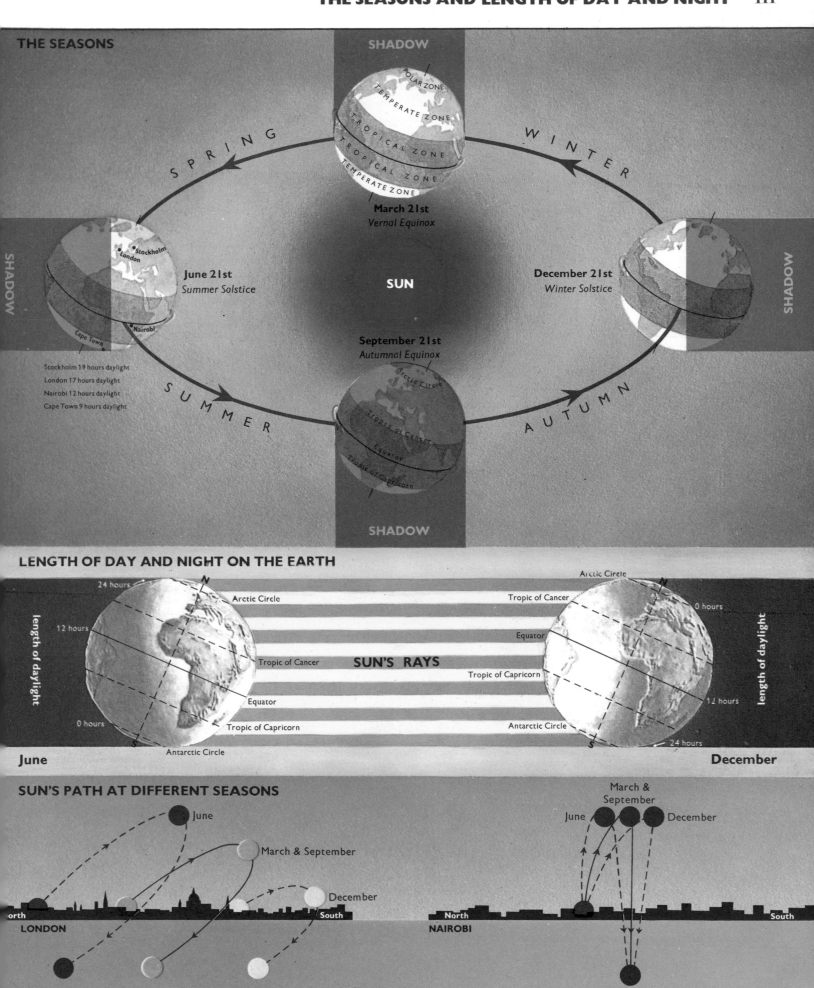

THE SEASONS

SHADOW

POLAR ZONE
TEMPERATE ZONE
TROPICAL ZONE
TROPICAL ZONE
TEMPERATE ZONE

March 21st
Vernal Equinox

SPRING

WINTER

Stockholm
London

June 21st
Summer Solstice

SUN

December 21st
Winter Solstice

SHADOW

Nairobi

SHADOW

Cape Town

Stockholm 19 hours daylight
London 17 hours daylight
Nairobi 12 hours daylight
Cape Town 9 hours daylight

SUMMER

AUTUMN

September 21st
Autumnal Equinox

Arctic Circle

Tropic of Cancer

Equator

Tropic of Capricorn

SHADOW

LENGTH OF DAY AND NIGHT ON THE EARTH

24 hours
N
Arctic Circle
length of daylight
12 hours
Tropic of Cancer
SUN'S RAYS
Equator
0 hours
Tropic of Capricorn
S
Antarctic Circle

Arctic Circle
N
Tropic of Cancer
0 hours
Equator
length of daylight
Tropic of Capricorn
12 hours
Antarctic Circle
S
24 hours

June

December

SUN'S PATH AT DIFFERENT SEASONS

June
March & September
December

North
South

LONDON

West

March & September
June
December

North
South

NAIROBI

West

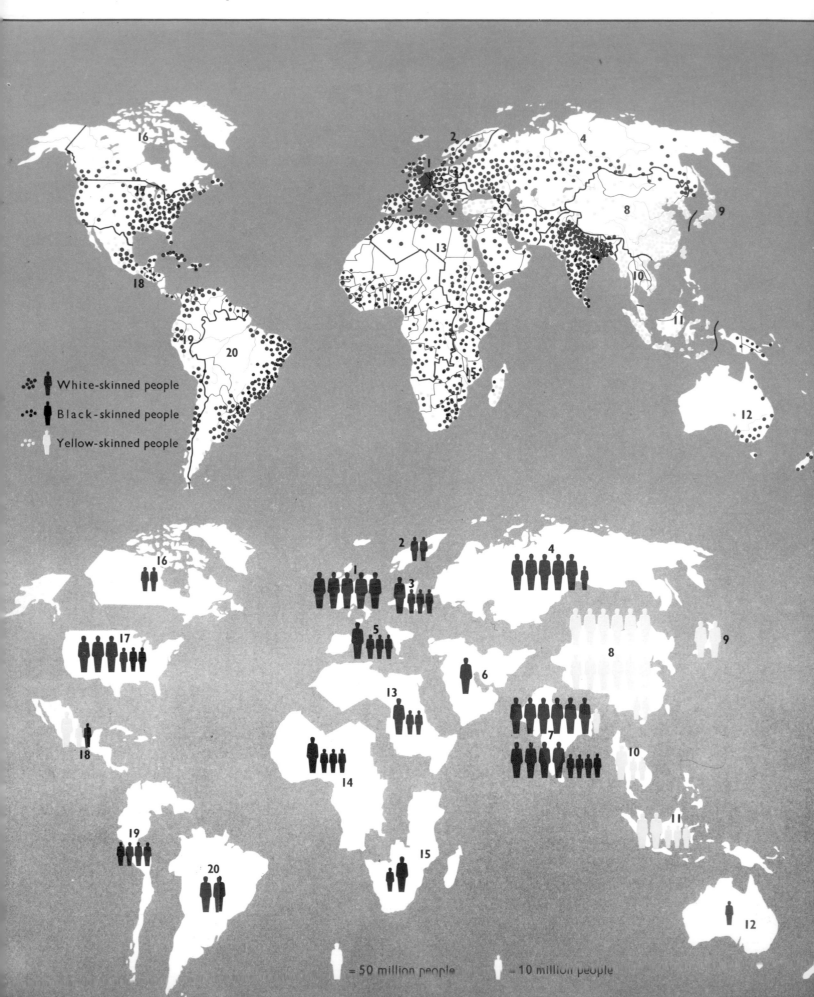

= 50 million people   = 10 million people

Legend:
White-skinned people
Black-skinned people
Yellow-skinned people

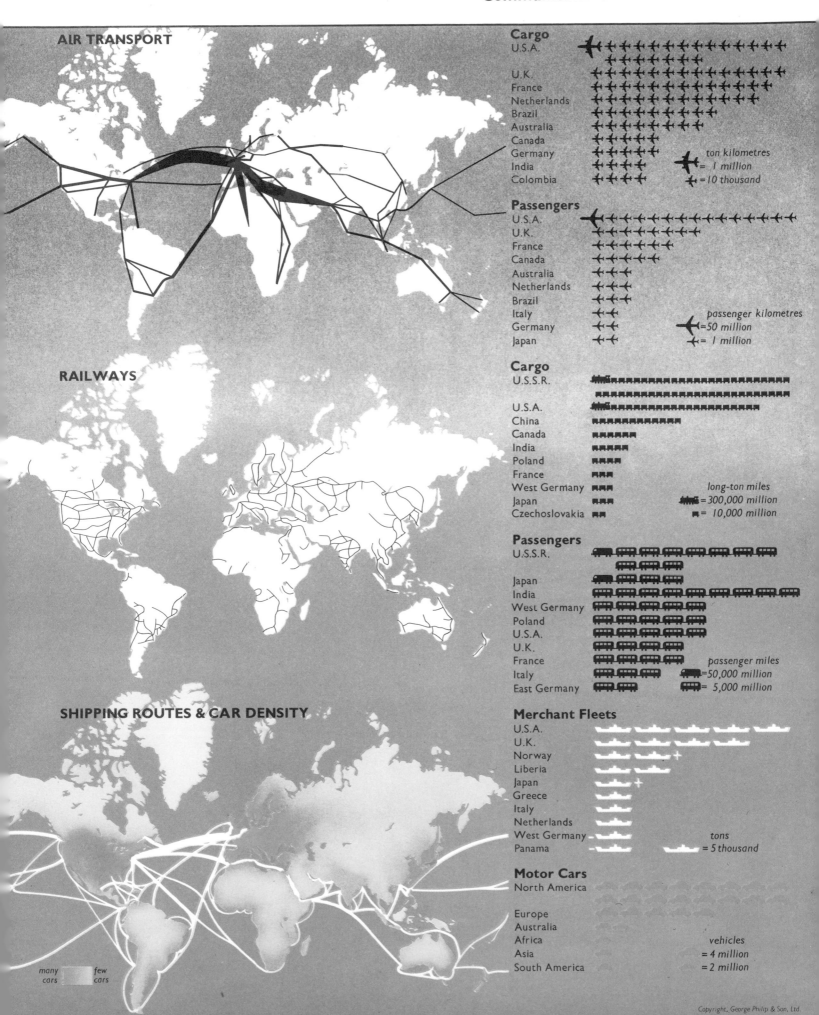

AIR TRANSPORT

Cargo
U.S.A.
U.K.
France
Netherlands
Brazil
Australia
Canada
Germany
India
Colombia

ton kilometres
= 1 million
= 10 thousand

Passengers
U.S.A.
U.K.
France
Canada
Australia
Netherlands
Brazil
Italy
Germany
Japan

passenger kilometres
= 50 million
= 1 million

RAILWAYS

Cargo
U.S.S.R.
U.S.A.
China
Canada
India
Poland
France
West Germany
Japan
Czechoslovakia

long-ton miles
= 300,000 million
= 10,000 million

Passengers
U.S.S.R.
Japan
India
West Germany
Poland
U.S.A.
U.K.
France
Italy
East Germany

passenger miles
= 50,000 million
= 5,000 million

SHIPPING ROUTES & CAR DENSITY

Merchant Fleets
U.S.A.
U.K.
Norway
Liberia
Japan
Greece
Italy
Netherlands
West Germany
Panama

tons
= 5 thousand

Motor Cars
North America

Europe
Australia
Africa
Asia
South America

vehicles
= 4 million
= 2 million

many cars   few cars

Copyright, George Philip & Son, Ltd.

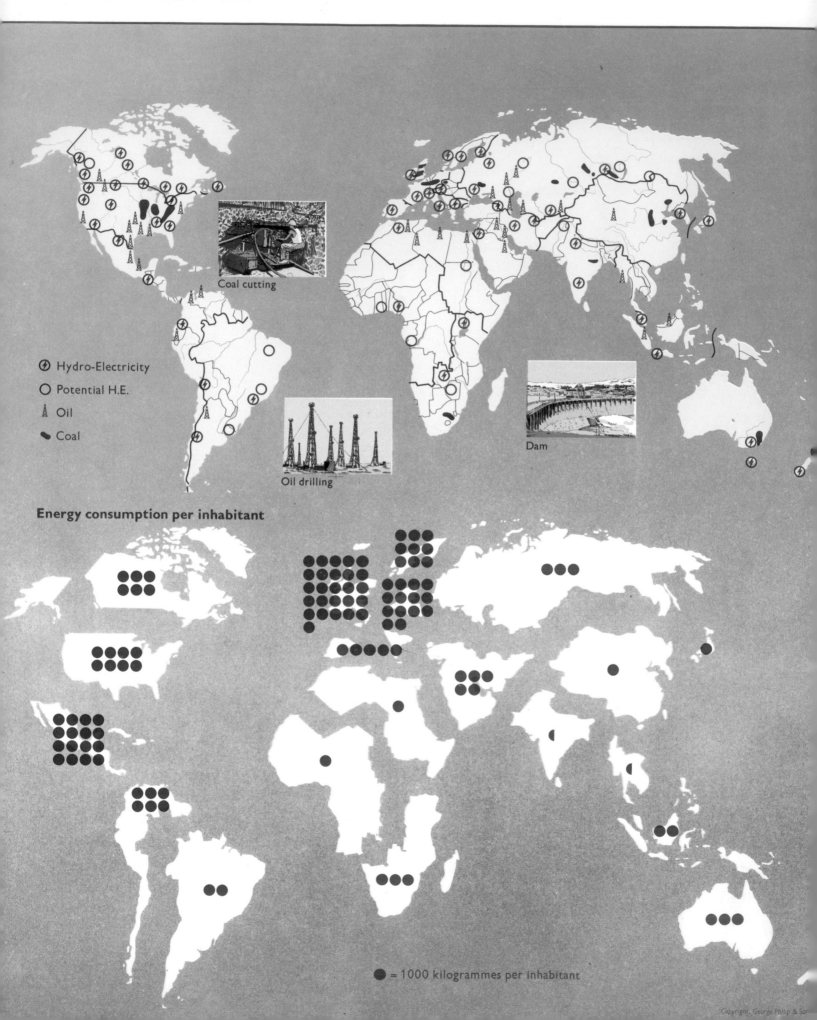

Coal cutting

Hydro-Electricity
Potential H.E.
Oil
Coal

Oil drilling

Dam

Energy consumption per inhabitant

= 1000 kilogrammes per inhabitant

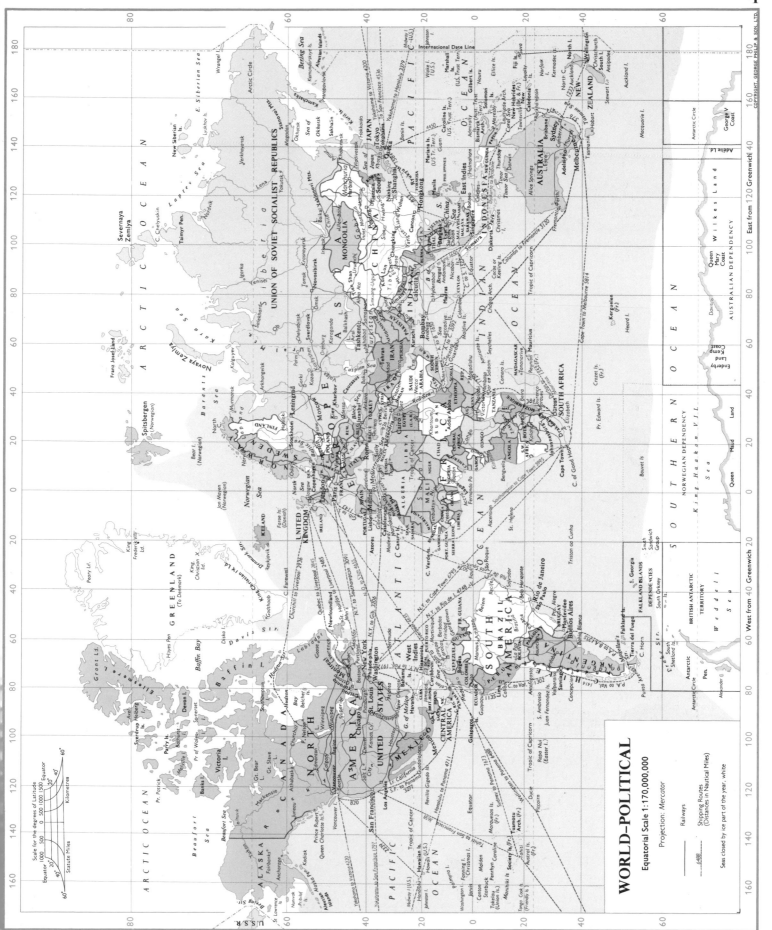

WORLD–POLITICAL

Equatorial Scale 1:170,000,000

Projection: Mercator

Railways

Shipping Routes
(Distances in Nautical Miles)

6488

Seas closed by ice part of the year, white

1

2

EUROPE

Scale 1:20,000,000 (320 Statute Miles = 1 inch)

100   0   100   200   300   400 Miles
100 0   200   400   600 Km.

Projection: Bonne

───── Principal Railways   ┈┈┈┈ Canals
_508_ Shipping Routes (Distances in Nautical Miles)
• 5377 Heights in feet

West 5 from Greenwich 0   5   East from 10 Greenwich   15   20   25   30

ICELAND

ARCTIC OCEAN

Arctic Circle

NORTH SEA

ATLANTIC OCEAN

UNITED KINGDOM

IRELAND

BAY OF BISCAY

PORTUGAL
SPAIN
MADRID
Lisbon

MOROCCO   ALGERIA   TUNISIA

MEDITERRANEAN SEA

FRANCE
PARIS

BELGIUM
LONDON

NETHERLANDS
GERMANY
BERLIN

DENMARK
Copenhagen

NORWAY
Oslo

SWEDEN
Stockholm

FINLAND
Helsinki

BALTIC SEA

POLAND
Warsaw

CZECHOSLOVAKIA
Prague

AUSTRIA
VIENNA

SWITZERLAND
Bern

ITALY
ROME

HUNGARY
BUDAPEST

YUGOSLAVIA

RUMANIA
Bucharest

BULGARIA
Sofia

GREECE
Athens

ADRIATIC SEA

Tyrrhenian Sea

Ionian Sea

AEGEAN SEA

Crete

TURKEY

CYPRUS

ESTONIA
LATVIA
LITHUANIA

WHITE RUSSIA

RUSSIA
Leningrad
MOSCOW

UKRAINE

SOVIET UNION

BLACK SEA

U.A.R.
Cairo

LIBYA   EGYPT

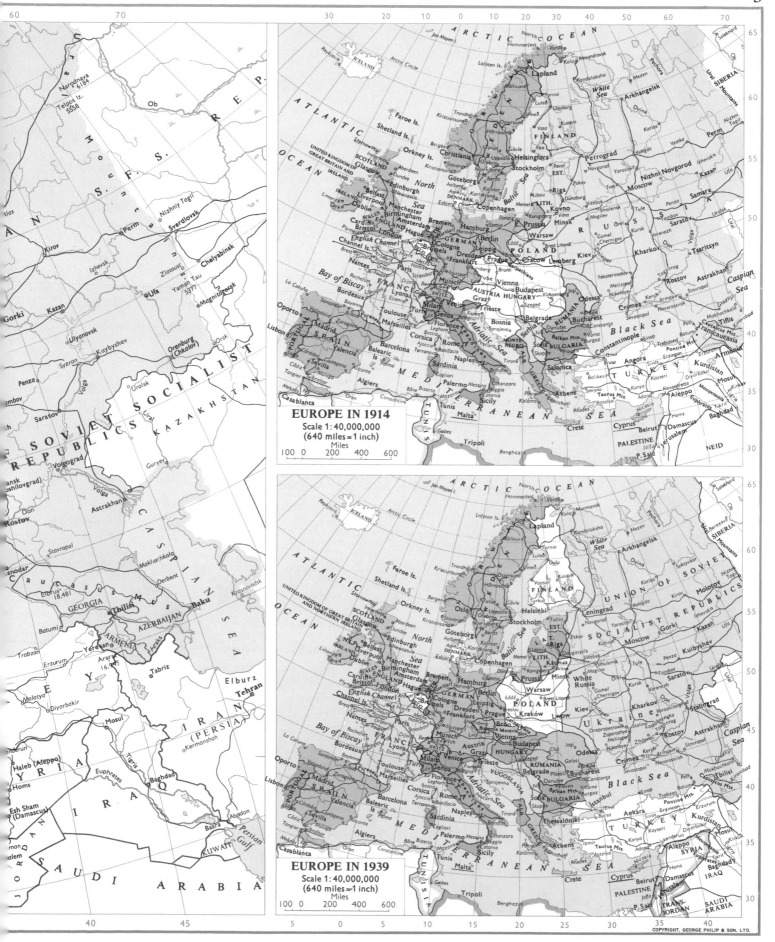

3

EUROPE IN 1914
Scale 1:40,000,000
(640 miles=1 inch)
Miles
100 0 200 400 600

EUROPE IN 1939
Scale 1:40,000,000
(640 miles=1 inch)
Miles
100 0 200 400 600

COPYRIGHT. GEORGE PHILIP & SON. LTD.

ENGLAND AND WALES

Scale 1 : 3,000,000 (48 Statute Miles = 1 inch)

10   10   20   30   40   50   60   70   80   90 Miles
20   0   20   40   60   80   100   120   140 Km.

Projection : Conical with two standard parallels

—— Railways   .... Canals

2676   Heights in feet

- ⊡ Towns of over 500,000 inhabitants
- ◉   ,,   from 200,000–500,000
- ◉   ,,   ,,   100,000–200,000
- ⊙   ,,   ,,   50,000–100,000
- ○   ,,   ,,   10,000–50,000
- ○   ,,   of under 10,000 inhabitants

West from Greenwich   0   East from Greenwich

COPYRIGHT. GEORGE PHILIP & SON, LTD.

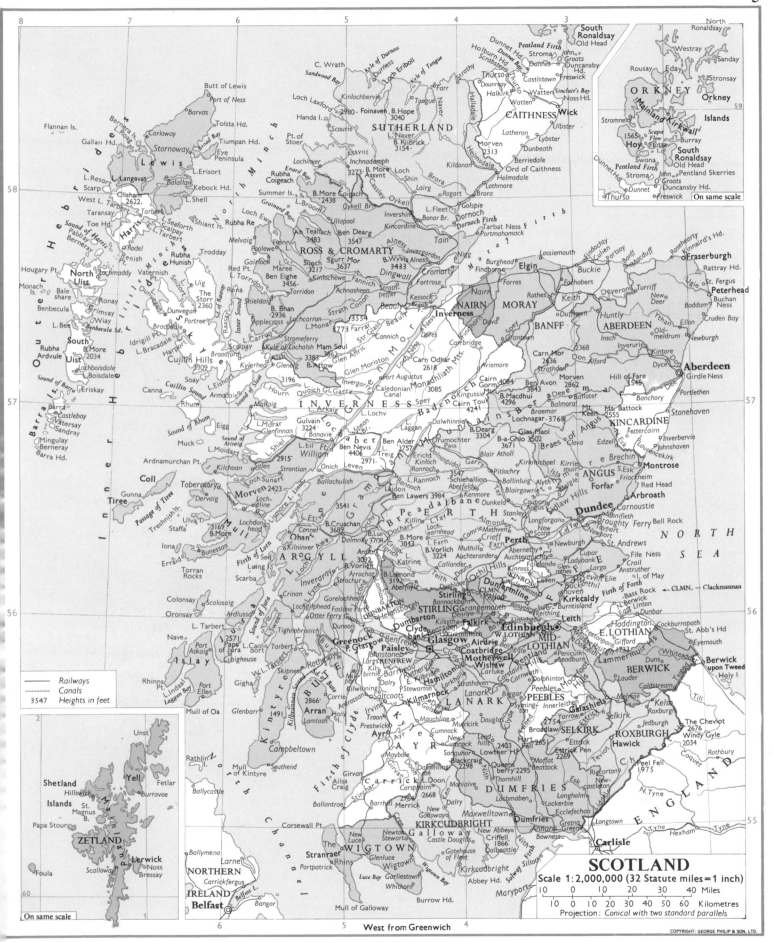

SCOTLAND

Scale 1 : 2,000,000 (32 Statute miles = 1 inch)

Miles 10 0 10 20 30 40

Kilometres 10 0 10 20 30 40 50 60

Projection : Conical with two standard parallels

Railways
Canals
3547 Heights in feet

On same scale

West from Greenwich

COPYRIGHT: GEORGE PHILIP & SON, LTD.

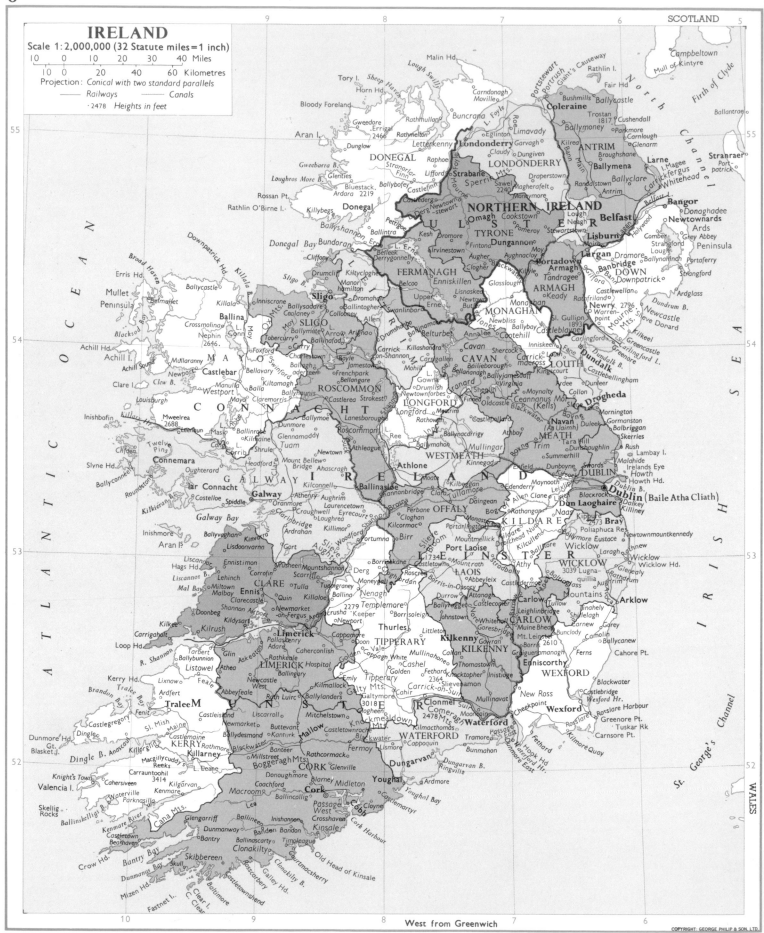

IRELAND
Scale 1:2,000,000 (32 Statute miles = 1 inch)
10   0   10   20   30   40 Miles
10   0   20   40   60 Kilometres
Projection: Conical with two standard parallels
— Railways .... Canals
· 2478 Heights in feet

West from Greenwich

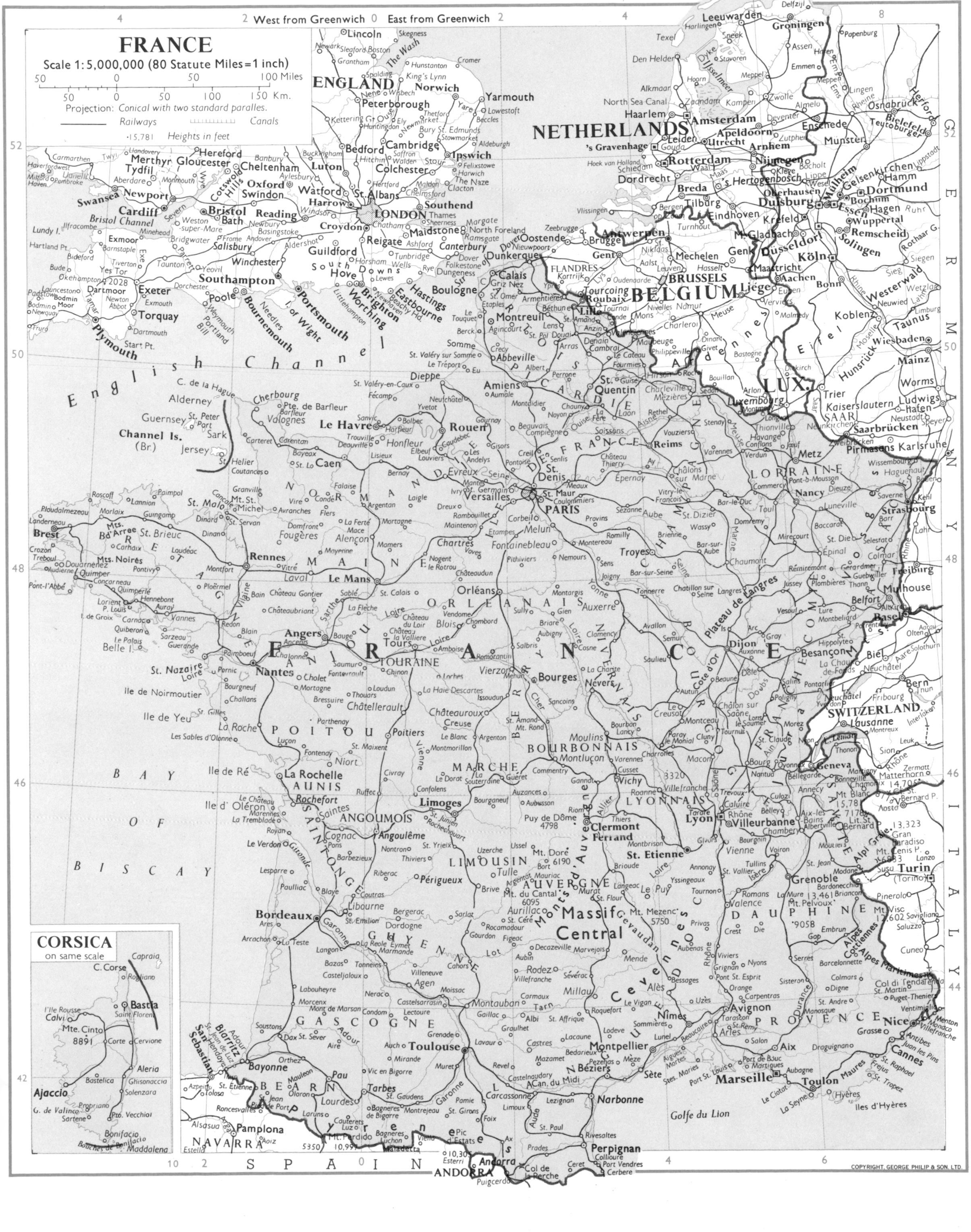

FRANCE

Scale 1:5,000,000 (80 Statute Miles=1 inch)

50 0 50 100 Miles
50 0 50 100 150 Km.

Projection: Conical with two standard parallels.

Railways   Canals

·15,781   Heights in feet

West from Greenwich   East from Greenwich

ENGLAND

NETHERLANDS

BELGIUM

LUX.

GERMANY

SWITZERLAND

ITALY

SPAIN

ANDORRA

F R A N C E

PARIS

BAY OF BISCAY

English Channel

Golfe du Lion

CORSICA
on same scale

Bastia
Ajaccio
Mte. Cinto 8891

COPYRIGHT. GEORGE PHILIP & SON LTD.

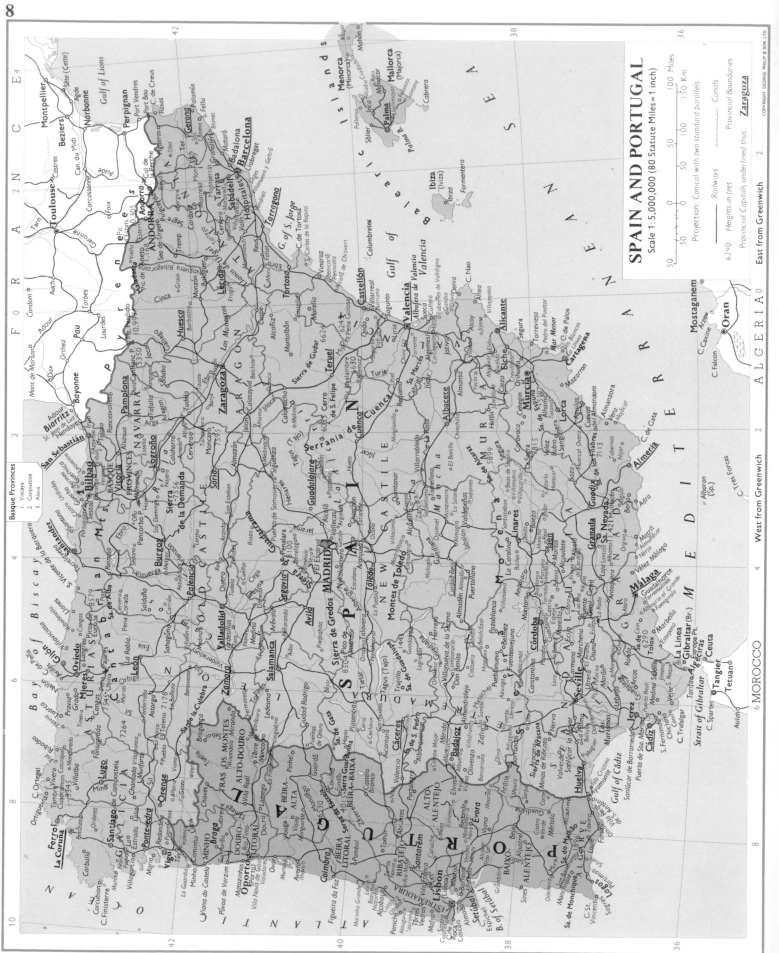

SPAIN AND PORTUGAL

Scale 1:5,000,000 (80 Statute Miles = 1 inch)

Projection: Conical with two standard parallels.

50	0	50 100 Miles
50	0	50 100 150 Km.

—— Railways   —·—· Canals

6290 Heights in feet   ----- Provincial Boundaries

Provincial Capitals underlined thus: **Zaragoza**

East from Greenwich   West from Greenwich

COPYRIGHT GEORGE PHILIP & SON, LTD.

Basque Provinces
1. Viscaya
2. Guipuzcoa
3. Alava

GERMANY & AUSTRIA

Scale 1:5,000,000 (80 Statute Miles=1 inch)

25 0   25   50   75   100 125 Miles

25 0   50   100   150   200 Km.

Projection : Conical with two standard parallels

——— Principal Railways   +++++++ Canals

4960 Heights in feet

COPYRIGHT. GEORGE PHILIP & SON. LTD

ITALY AND THE BALKAN STATES
Scale 1:5,000,000 (80 Statute Miles = 1 inch)

Projection: Conical with two standard parallels.

Railways   Canals   6017 Heights in feet

CRETE
on same scale

RUMANIA

GOSLAVIA (YUGOSLAVIA)

BULGARIA

U.S.S.R.

NGARY (HUNGARY)

ALBANIA

GREECE

THRACE

MACEDONIA

Transylvania

Transylvanian Alps

Carpathians

Wallachia

Banat

SERBIA

CRNA GORA (MONTENEGRO)

Kosovo-Metohija

Balkan Mountains (Stara Planina)

Rhodope Mountains

EPIRUS

THESSALY

PELOPONNESE

KIKLÁDHES (Cyclades)

N. SPORADES

DODECANESE

BLACK SEA

Sea of Marmara

IONIAN SEA

AEGEAN SEA

Str. of Otranto

Gulf of Corinth

Dardanelles (Hellespont)

Bosporus

Istrança Mts.

Major cities: Bucharest (Bucureşti), Belgrade (Beograd), Sofia, Athens (Athinai), Thessaloniki, Bitolj (Monastir), Skoplje, Tiranë, Sarajevo, Novi Sad, Timişoara, Craiova, Ploeşti, Braşov, Cluj, Oradea, Arad, Szeged, Galaţi, Brăila, Constanţa, Varna, Burgas, Ploydiv, Edirne, Istanbul, Izmir (Smyrna), Bursa, Pátrai, Vólos, Lárisa, Kérkira (Corfu), Brindisi, Lecce

Mt. Olympus 9550, Mt. Athos 6670, Musala 9596, Rila Pl., Peleaga 8268, Moldoveanu 8346, Mt. Omul 8222

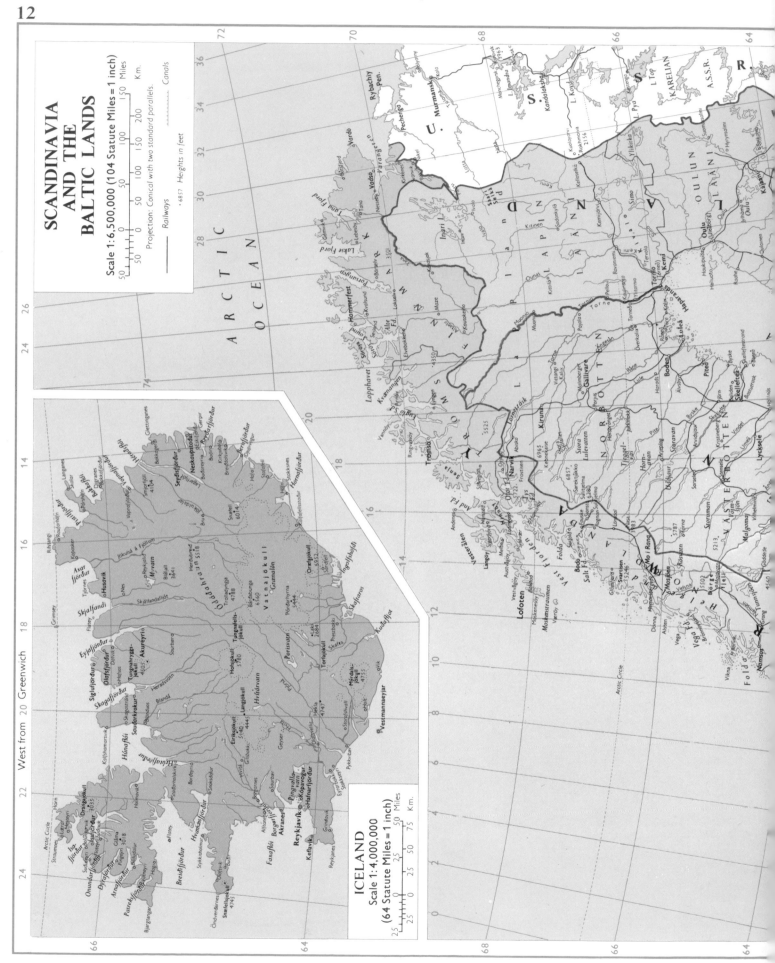

East from 18 Greenwich

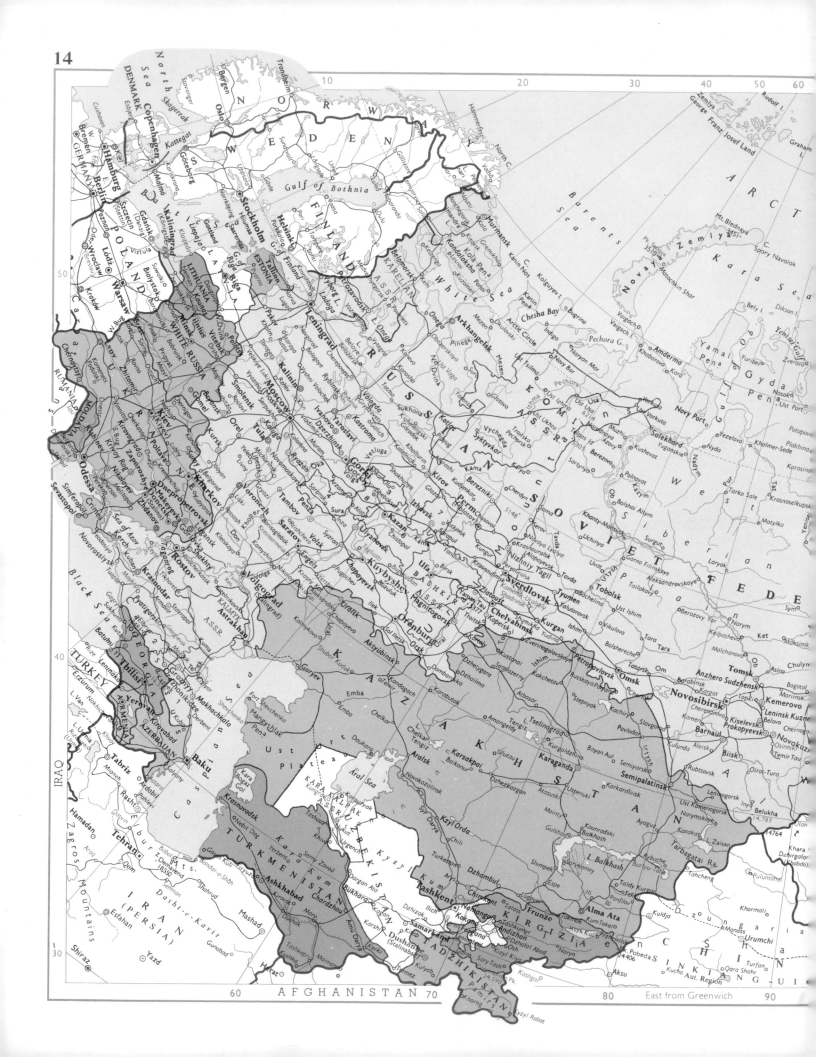

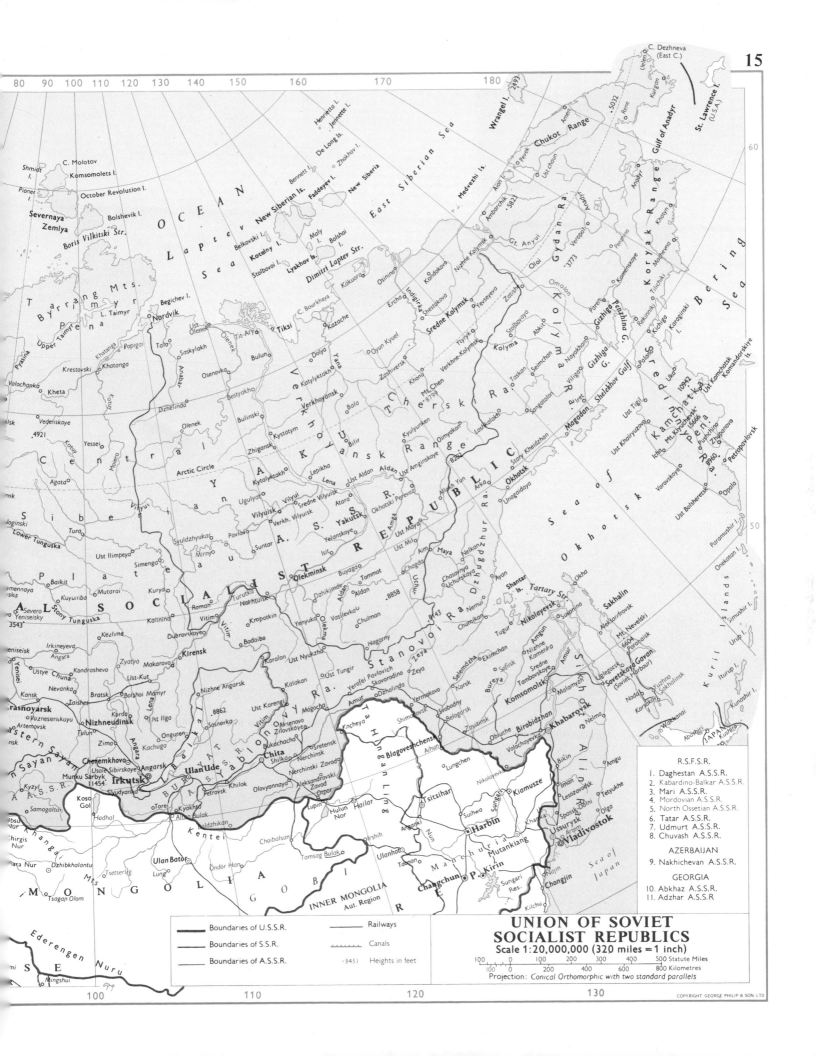

UNION OF SOVIET SOCIALIST REPUBLICS

Scale 1:20,000,000 (320 miles = 1 inch)

Projection: Conical Orthomorphic with two standard parallels

	Boundaries of U.S.S.R.			Railways
	Boundaries of S.S.R.			Canals
	Boundaries of A.S.S.R.			·3451 Heights in feet

100 0 100 200 300 400 500 Statute Miles
800 Kilometres

R.S.F.S.R.
1. Daghestan A.S.S.R.
2. Kabardino-Balkar A.S.S.R.
3. Mari A.S.S.R.
4. Mordovian A.S.S.R.
5. North Ossetian A.S.S.R.
6. Tatar A.S.S.R.
7. Udmurt A.S.S.R.
8. Chuvash A.S.S.R.

AZERBAIJAN
9. Nakhichevan A.S.S.R.

GEORGIA
10. Abkhaz A.S.S.R.
11. Adzhar A.S.S.R.

16

ASIA

Scale 1:40,000,000 (640 Statute Miles = 1 inch)

400 200 0   400   800 Miles
600 400 200 0   400   800   1200 Km.

Projection: Bonne

——————— Principal Railways

——4536—— Shipping Routes (Distances in Nautical Miles)

East from 80 Greenwich

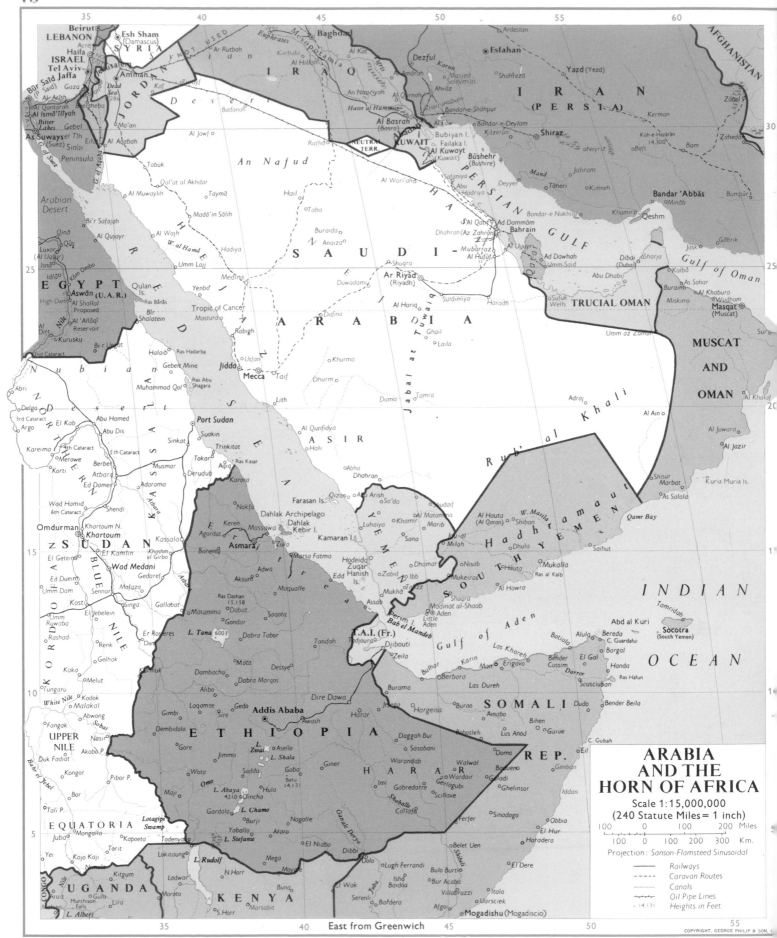

ARABIA AND THE HORN OF AFRICA

Scale 1:15,000,000
(240 Statute Miles = 1 inch)

100   0   100   200 Miles
100   0   100   200   300 Km.

Projection: Sanson-Flamsteed Sinusoidal

Railways
Caravan Routes
Canals
Oil Pipe Lines
·14,131   Heights in Feet

East from Greenwich

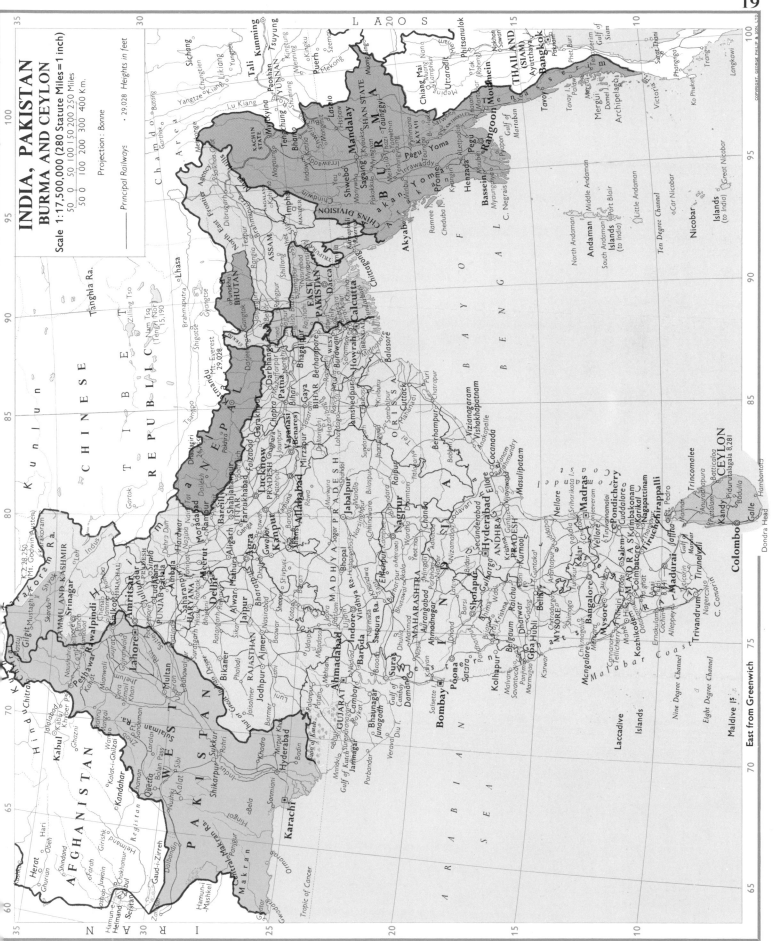

INDIA, PAKISTAN BURMA AND CEYLON

Scale 1:17,500,000 (280 Statute Miles=1 inch)

Projection : Bonne

Principal Railways   • 29,028 Heights in feet

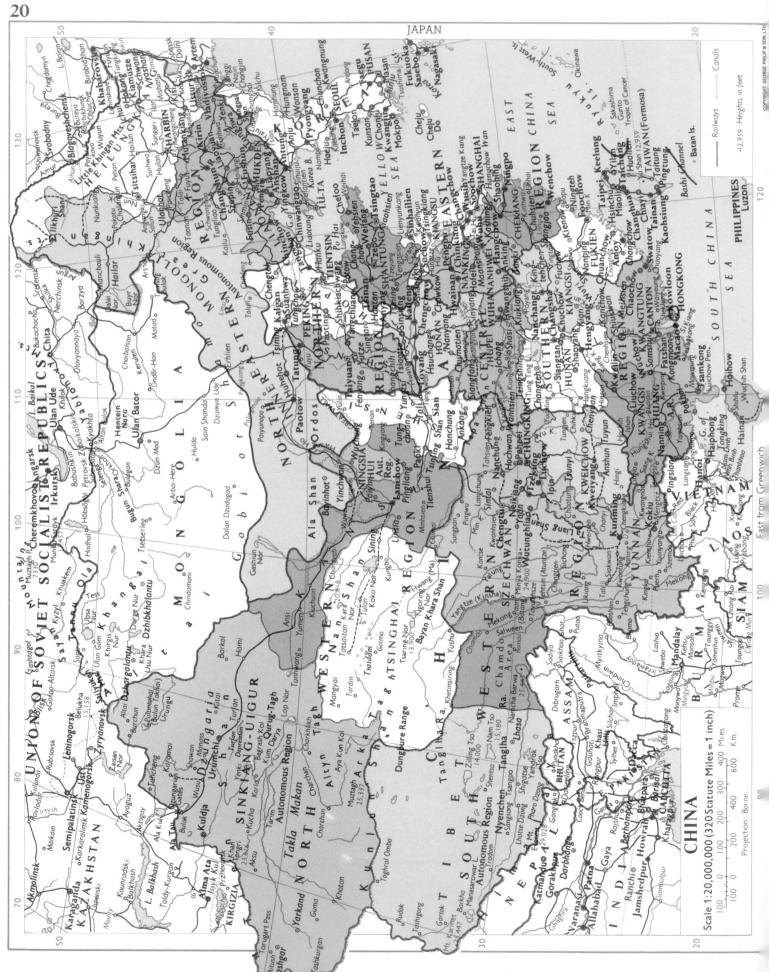

CHINA

Scale 1:20,000,000 (320 Statute Miles = 1 inch)

Projection: Borne.

| Railways |
| Canals |
| -12,959 Heights in feet |

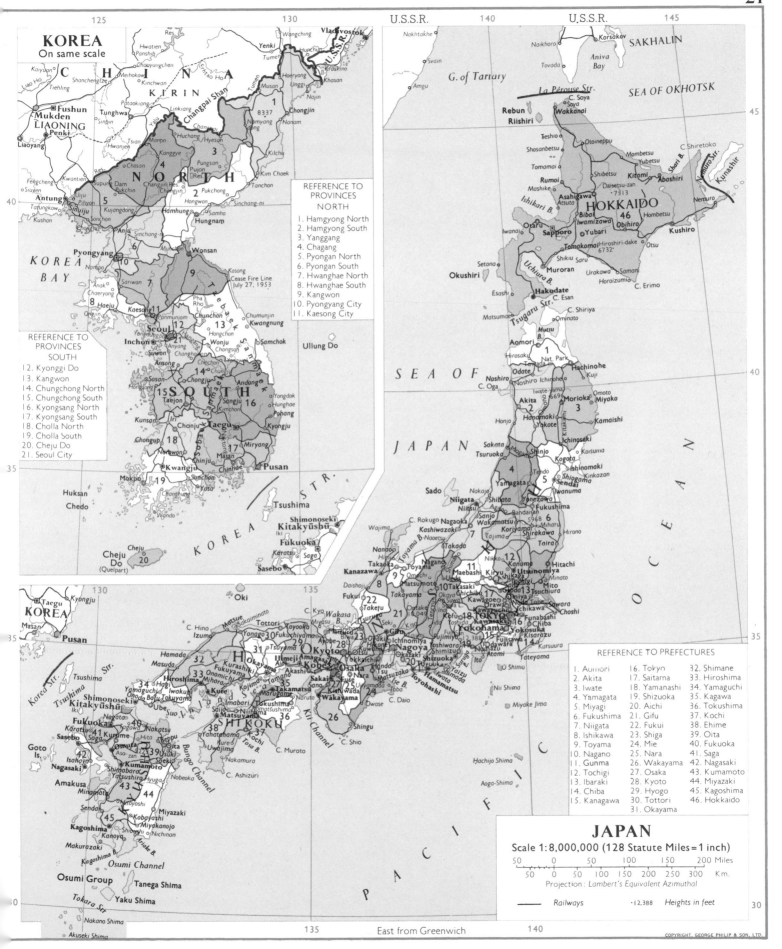

KOREA
On same scale

REFERENCE TO PROVINCES NORTH

1. Hamgyong North
2. Hamgyong South
3. Yanggang
4. Chagang
5. Pyongan North
6. Pyongan South
7. Hwanghae North
8. Hwanghae South
9. Kangwon
10. Pyongyang City
11. Kaesong City

REFERENCE TO PROVINCES SOUTH

12. Kyonggi Do
13. Kangwon
14. Chungchong North
15. Chungchong South
16. Kyongsang North
17. Kyongsang South
18. Cholla North
19. Cholla South
20. Cheju Do
21. Seoul City

REFERENCE TO PREFECTURES

1. Aomori	16. Tokyo	32. Shimane
2. Akita	17. Saitama	33. Hiroshima
3. Iwate	18. Yamanashi	34. Yamaguchi
4. Yamagata	19. Shizuoka	35. Kagawa
5. Miyagi	20. Aichi	36. Tokushima
6. Fukushima	21. Gifu	37. Kochi
7. Niigata	22. Fukui	38. Ehime
8. Ishikawa	23. Shiga	39. Oita
9. Toyama	24. Mie	40. Fukuoka
10. Nagano	25. Nara	41. Saga
11. Gunma	26. Wakayama	42. Nagasaki
12. Tochigi	27. Osaka	43. Kumamoto
13. Ibaraki	28. Kyoto	44. Miyazaki
14. Chiba	29. Hyogo	45. Kagoshima
15. Kanagawa	30. Tottori	46. Hokkaido
	31. Okayama	

JAPAN
Scale 1:8,000,000 (128 Statute Miles=1 inch)

50   0   50   100   150   200 Miles
50   0   50 100 150 200 250 300 Km.

Projection: Lambert's Equivalent Azimuthal

———— Railways   ·12,388 Heights in feet

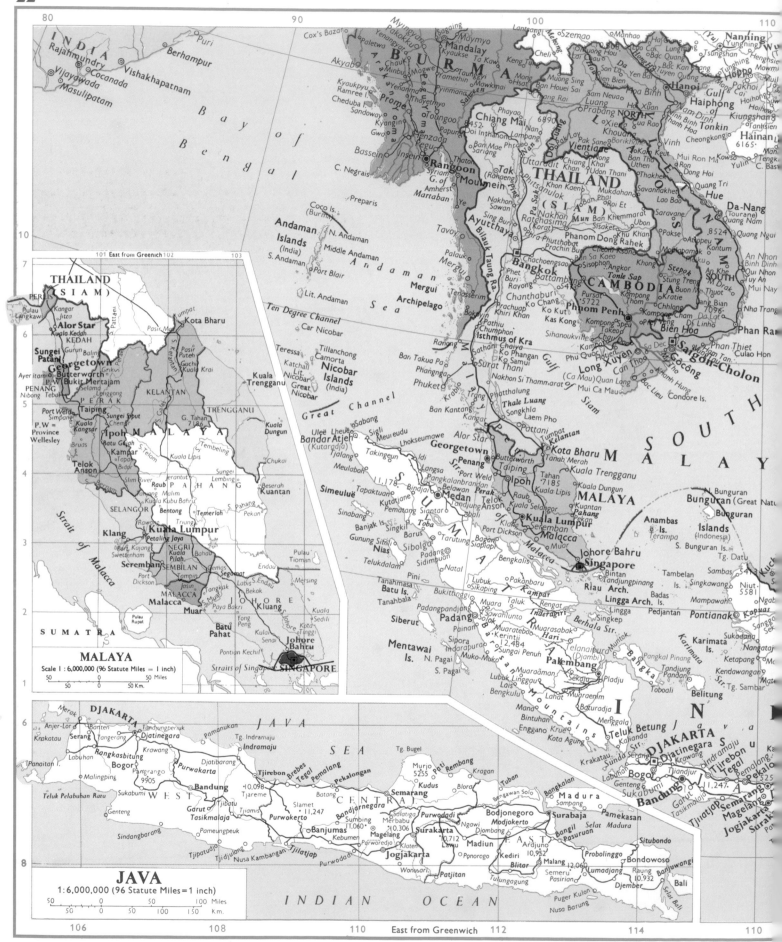

80

90

100

110

INDIA

Rajahmundry
Vijayawada
Cocanada
Masulipatam
Vishakhapatnam

Berhampur

Puri

Cox's Bazar

B a y   o f

B e n g a l

C. Negrais

Preparis

Coco Is.
(Burma)

Andaman
Islands
(India)

N. Andaman

Middle Andaman

S. Andaman

Port Blair

A n d a m a n

S e a

BURMA

Myingyan
Pakokku
Chauk
Yenangyaung
Minbu
Prome
Henzada
Bassein
Insein
Rangoon
Syriam
Moulmein

Akyab
Kyaukpyu
Ramree I.
Cheduba I.
Sandoway
Gwa
Kyangin

Magwe
Pyinmana
Yamethin

Maymyo
Mandalay
Kyaukse
Meiktila
Toungoo
Pegu

Sagaing
Shwebo
Ye-u

Mong Mit
Lashio
Hsat

Keng Tung

Chiang Rai
Chiang Mai

G. of
Martaban

Thaton

Ye

Tavoy

Mergui

Tenasserim

Mergui
Archipelago

8452
Doi Inthanon

THAILAND
(SIAM)

Nakhon
Sawan

Ayutthaya

Bangkok
Chachoengsao

Chanthaburi

Isthmus of Kra

Chumphon

Surat Thani

Nakhon Si Thammarat

Phuket

Songkhla

Pattani

Georgetown
Penang

Ten Degree Channel

Car Nicobar

Teressa
Camorta
Katchall
Lit.
Nicobar
Great
Nicobar

Nicobar
Islands
(India)

Great Channel

SOUTH   MALAY

SUMATRA

Bandar Atjeh
(Kutaradja)

Medan

Padang

Palembang

JAVA   SEA

DJAKARTA

INDIAN   OCEAN

Inset map — MALAYA:

THAILAND
(SIAM)

PERLIS
Kangar
Pulau
Langkawi
Alor Star
KEDAH
Sungei
Patani
Georgetown
Butterworth
Bukit Mertajam
PENANG
Taiping
PERAK
Ipoh   MALAYA
Kampar
Telok
Anson
KELANTAN
Kota Bharu
Kuala Krai
TRENGGANU
Kuala
Trengganu
G. Tahan
Kuala Lipis
PAHANG
Kuala
Dungun
Chukai
Kuantan
SELANGOR
Klang
Kuala Lumpur
Petaling Jaya
NEGRI
SEMBILAN
Seremban
Port
Dickson
Tampin
MALACCA
Malacca
Muar
JOHORE
Kluang
Batu
Pahat
Johore
Bahru
SINGAPORE
SUMATRA
Strait of Malacca

MALAYA

Scale 1 : 6,000,000 (96 Statute Miles = 1 inch)

50   0   50 Miles
50   0   50 Km.

Inset map — JAVA:

DJAKARTA
Serang
Tangerang
Bogor
Bandung
Tjirebon
Tegal
Pekalongan
Semarang
Surakarta
Jogjakarta
Surabaja
Madura
WEST   CENTRAL   EAST

JAVA

1 : 6,000,000 (96 Statute Miles = 1 inch)

50   0   50   100 Miles
50   0   50   100   150 Km.

INDIAN   OCEAN

106

108

110   East from Greenwich   112

114

110

EAST INDIES
AND
FURTHER INDIA
Scale 1:17,000,000 (272 Statute miles=1 inch)

50 0   100   200   300   400   500 Miles
100 0   100 200 300 400 500 600 700 800 Km.

Projection: Conical

———— Railways   ———— Canals
9612 Heights in feet   —·—· Oil Pipe Lines

Canton Waiyeung Swatow Tainan Formosa (Taiwan)
Namhoi Tungkun Kityang Kityeilai Taitung
Sumwuio Kowloon Kaohsiung Lü Tao (Huoshao Tao)
Macao Victoria Pingtung Hengchun Hungt'ou Hsü (Lan Hsü)
Yeungkong Hong Kong Bashi Channel Y'Ami
(British) Pratas (China) Batan Bascoe Batan Is.
Balintang Balintang Channel
Paracel Is. Scarborough Babuyan Is.
(China) Shoal Aparri
Laoag Bangued
Batac Tuguegarao
Vigan Solano Palanan
San Fernando 9612 Casiguran
Lingayen Baguio San Ildefonso
C. Bolinao Dagupan San Jose C.
Lingayen G. Cabanatuan
Iba Tarlac Quezon City PHILIPPINES
San Fernando Manila Daet Yog Pt.
Bataan San Pablo Calauag Catanduanes
Manila Bay Cavite Naga Virac
Lubang Is. Lucena Sorsogon Gubat
Botangas Boac Bulan Calbayog
Mindoro Legaspi Samar
Mindoro Str. Masbate Catbalogan
Calamian Group Looc Roxas Tacloban
Busuanga Cuyo Pandan Ormoc Leyte
Palawan Is. Iloi Panay Cebu Baybay
West York San Jose Bacolod Bohol Dinagat
Thitu Dumaran Negros Siargao
Discovery Reefs Bacuit Tanjay Dipolog Tandag
Fiery Cross Reef Taytay Cagayan Is. Surigao
Sin Cowe Puerto Princesa Dumaguete Butuan Lianga
(Phil.) Tubbataha Mindanao Cagayan San Juan
London Reefs Reefs Dipolog Talisayon Malaybalay
Islands Mt. Mantalingajan Mandih Mindanao
Spratly I. 6839 Sulu Sea Liloy Ozamiz Davao
(Br.) Investigator Shoal Bancoran Pagadian Cotabato Apo Mati
Amboyna Cay Bugsuk San Miguel Is. Dulawan 9690 Digos
(Br.) Balabac Cagayan Zamboanga C. San Agustin
Louisa Reef Balembangan Sulu Basilan Luan Glan
conia Kudat Pangutaran Lamitan Basilan Kiambo Sarangani Is.
shoals Banggi Group Jolo Tinaca Pt. Nenusa Is.
Kota Kinabalu Labuk B. Turtle Is. Sulu Arch. Beo Talaud Is.
Kinabalu Sandakan Tawitawi Karakelong
I A Victoria 13,455 Pintasan Lahad Datu Tahuna
Brunei Papar Melalap (N. BORNEO) Sibutu Sangihe
Labuan Beaufort Weston SABAH Tawau Sangihe Is.
BRUNEI Muara St. Lucia B. Celebes Siau
Tg. Baram Limbang Bunju Morotai
Miri Marudi Belait Tarakan Manado Pitu MAPIA IS.
Mitkah Malinau Tandjung Selor Klabat Galela Asia Is. NEW GUINEA
aya Bintulu Longleju Kajan Maratua 6545 Djailolo Aju Is. Equator Manokwari Schouten
Sibu SARAWAK Lnngnawan 6736 Maju Ternate Gotowasi Waigeo Numfoor Supiori Biak Is.
Simanggang Kapit Kong Kemuh Kuandang Weda Patuni Mios Num Bosnek
Nangabadau 587/3 Mahakam 6562 Tg. Mangkalihat Amurang Halmahera Waibeem Wakre Sorong 9842 Japen
Putussibau Muller Mts. Batuputilih Tolitoli Gorontalo Molucca Klamono Vogel Wersar kop Wariap Serui
itau BORNEO 7474 6430 Buol Paleleh Buli Sea Samate Sege Jambe Mogoi Windehsi
gapinoh KALIMANTAN Schwaner 8881 Labuha Semo Misoöl Saga Babo Geelvink
Kualakurun Mts. Tinombo Tilamuta Batjan McCluer G. Bula Fakfak Kaimana WEST Bay
Puruktjau Muara-Antjalung Gulf of Togian Is. Obi Weri IRIAN Kiruru
G Sampit Tenggarong Bontang Tomini (Penju) Obi Is. Ceram Sea Karufa Wanapiri
Tannhgrogot Samarinda Donggala Parigi Gani Sawai Wahai C e r a m
r Kualakapuas Pasangkaju Palu Uebonti Luwuk Peleng Sanana Piru Tehoru Gorong I.
e Sampit Bay Barito Balikpapan Lariang Poso Banggai Taliabu Sula Is. Wamlang Namlea Ambon Geser Gorong
a apembuang t Tandjung SULAWESI G. of Mangole Buru Leksula Saparua Bandanaira Watubela Is. Adi
Kandangan o Balangan (Celebes) Tolo Banggai Is. Ambelau Ambon Banda Is. Ewab Is. (Kai) Dobo Wokam
Bandjarmasin Kotabaru L. Masamba Manui A Banda Sea Tual Banda Elat Aru
O Sebuku Palopo Towuti Wowoni Kai Ketjil Trangan Kobroor
N Kintap Laut 11,335 Rantekombola Salabangka Is. Penju Is. Mahuk South Daja Is.
Pelaihari Madjene Kolaka Kendari Lucipara Is. Tanimbar
E Kuala Ketjil Is. Masalima Is. Parepare Buapinang Serua Larat Is.
Karamian Sebulu Maros Gulf of Butung Gunungapi West Daja Is. Jamdena
S Bawean Salembu Watansoppeng Makasar Bone Wangiwangi Nila Saumlaki
Salajar Kadjang Muna Tukangbesi Is. Teun South Daja Is.
I Tg. Selatan Pelaihari Kabaena Binongko Damar Tepa Babar
Postiljon Is. Bonthain Pasarwadjo Masela Tanimbar
a Kangean Is. (Benteng) Salajar Wetar Str. Wetar Roma Nikini
als Balabalangan Takalar Kalaotoa West Daja Is. Sermata Selaru Arafura
Sumenep Tanahdjampea Iwaki Kisar Moa Masela
Surabaja Pamekasan Flores Sea Larantuka Atauro (Port.) Nova Sagres C. Van Diemen Coburg Sea
Madura Sitybondo 0.308 Reo Adonara Alor Dili Vila Nova de Malaca Pen. Goulburn Is.
Kedri Malang Pasuruan Singaradja 2,224 Maumere Lomblen Pantar 9678 Macau (Va. Salazar) Melville
12,060 Rindjani Mojo 9353 Geliting Paloe Atapupu (Port.) I. Darwin
Bali Lumadjung Matoram 7874 Ende Pariti AMBENO Armindo Monteiro Van Diemen Pine Creek
Djember Penida Sumbawabesar Rateng (Port.) Oussi Nikini G. Bathurst AUSTRALIA
Banjuwangi Lombok Sumbawa Waingapu Sawu Sea Kupang Timor Daly Katherine
Denpasar Lunjuk-besar Memboro Melolo Seba Roti Sea C. Van Diemen Matranka
Lombok Waikabubak Sumba 4019 Sawu Is. Baä Timor Sea Bathurst Birdum

Si Luzon Strait
CHINA SEA
PACIFIC OCEAN
Yap Is.
Ngulu Atoll
Palau Koror Caroline Is. (U.S. Trust Terr.)
Palau Is.
Sonsorol Is.
Pulo Anna Merir
Tobi
Mapia Is.
Japen
Numfoor Biak Is.
Wokam Aru

CELEBES Sea
BORNEO
KALIMANTAN
SARAWAK
SULAWESI (Celebes)
Makassar Str.
Java Sea
INDONESIA
Lesser Sunda Islands
Flores Sawu Sea
INDIAN OCEAN
TIMOR SEA

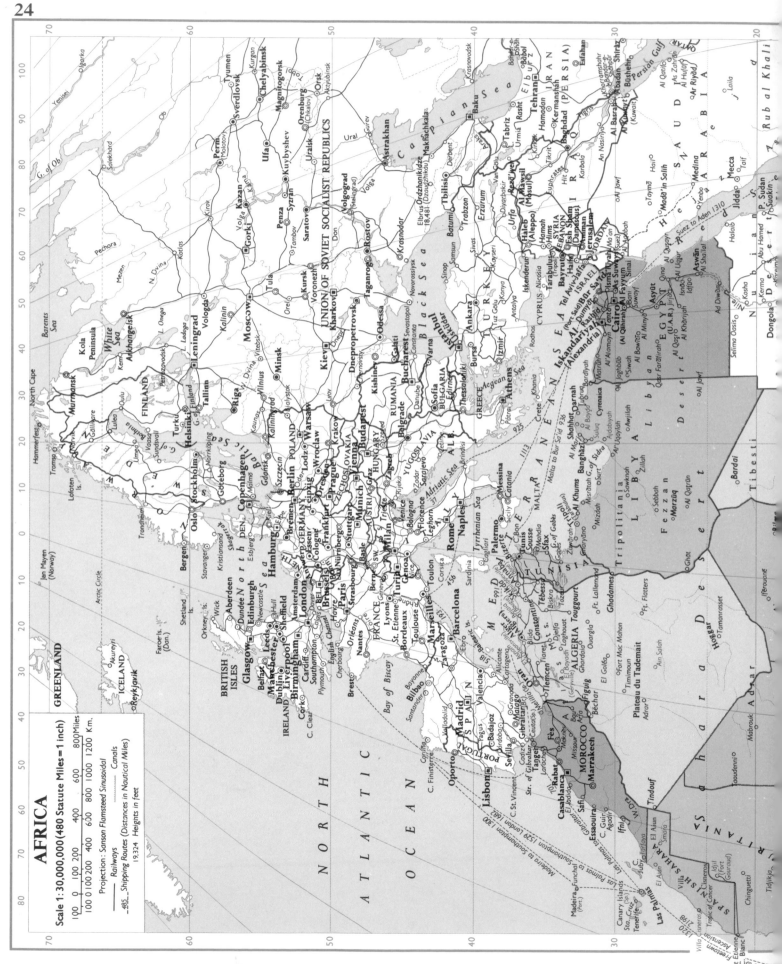

AFRICA

Scale 1:30,000,000 (480 Statute Miles=1 inch)

100 0 100 200   400   600   800 Miles
100 0 100 200 400 600 800 1000 1200 Km.

Projection: Sanson Flamsteed Sinusoidal

—— Railways
—485— Shipping Routes (Distances in Nautical Miles)
———— Canals

19,324 Heights in feet

GREENLAND

ICELAND
Reykjavik

UNION OF SOVIET SOCIALIST REPUBLICS

BRITISH ISLES

FINLAND

SWEDEN

NORWAY

DEN.

GERMANY

POLAND

CZECHOSLOVAKIA

AUSTRIA

HUNGARY

FRANCE

SPAIN

PORTUGAL

ITALY

YUGOSLAVIA

ALB.

RUMANIA

BULGARIA

GREECE

TURKEY

SYRIA

LEBANON

ISRAEL

JORDAN

CYPRUS

IRAQ

IRAN (PERSIA)

SAUDI ARABIA

EGYPT (U.A.R.)

LIBYA

Tripolitania

Fezzan

Cyrenaica

TUNISIA

ALGERIA

MOROCCO

SPANISH SAHARA

MAURITANIA

Sahara Desert

Libyan Desert

Nubian Desert

Arabian Desert

NORTH ATLANTIC OCEAN

North Sea

Baltic Sea

Mediterranean Sea

Black Sea

Caspian Sea

Aegean Sea

Adriatic Sea

Tyrrhenian Sea

Persian Gulf

Red Sea

Ar Rub' al Khali

QATAR

SOUTH YEMEN · YEMEN · SOMALI REP. · ETHIOPIA · ERITREA · SUDAN · CHAD · NIGER · MALI · SENEGAL · GAMBIA · PORT. GUINEA · GUINEA · SIERRA LEONE · LIBERIA · IVORY COAST · UPPER VOLTA · GHANA · TOGO · DAHOMEY · NIGERIA · CAMEROON · CENTRAL AFRICA · GABON · CONGO · CONGO · ANGOLA · ZAMBIA · RHODESIA · MALAWI · MOZAMBIQUE · TANZANIA · KENYA · UGANDA · RWANDA · BURUNDI · KATANGA · BOTSWANA · SOUTH WEST AFRICA · SOUTH AFRICA · TRANSVAAL · ORANGE FREE STATE · NATAL · LESOTHO · CAPE PROVINCE · MALAGASY REPUBLIC

Omdurman · Khartoum · El Dueim · El Obeid · El Fasher · Kassala · Kosti · Singa · Wad Medani · Juba · Wau · Bahr el Ghazal · Rumbek

Addis Ababa · Gondar · Dire Dawa · Harar · Amara · Asmara · Berbera · Hargeisa · Obbia · Mogadishu · Brava · Kismayu

Kampala · Entebbe · Nairobi · Mombasa & Kilindini · Kisumu · Eldoret · Kitale · L. Rudolf · L. Victoria · Kilimanjaro · Arusha · Mwanza · Tabora · Dodoma · Morogoro · Dar es Salaam · Tanga · Iringa · Mbeya

Kinshasa (Leopoldville) · Brazzaville · Libreville · Douala · Yaoundé · Bangui · Bangassou · Kisangani (Stanleyville) · Bukavu · Luluabourg · Albertville · Elisabethville · Mbandaka · Matadi · Boma · Cabinda · Banana

Luanda · Nova Lisboa · Lobito · Benguela · Moçâmedes · Malange · Carmona

Lusaka · Ndola · Livingstone · Bulawayo · Salisbury · Gwelo · Umtali · Victoria Falls

Pretoria · Johannesburg · Germiston · Kimberley · Bloemfontein · Pietermaritzburg · Durban · East London · Grahamstown · Port Elizabeth · Capetown · Mossel Bay · Walvis Bay · Swakopmund · Windhoek · Lüderitz · Keetmanshoop · Port Nolloth

Lagos · Ibadan · Kano · Kaduna · Zaria · Enugu · Port Harcourt · Benin City · Calabar · Maiduguri · Sokoto · Jos · Ilorin

Accra · Kumasi · Takoradi · Sekondi · Tamale · Abidjan · Bouaké · Bobo Dioulasso · Ouagadougou · Freetown · Monrovia · Conakry · Bamako · Dakar · St. Louis · Banjul

Lourenço Marques · Beira · Quelimane · Mozambique · Zomba · Blantyre

Tananarive · Tamatave · Majunga · Fianarantsoa · Tuléar

West from Greenwich · East from Greenwich

Tropic of Capricorn · Equator

ATLANTIC OCEAN · SOUTH ATLANTIC OCEAN · INDIAN OCEAN · Gulf of Guinea

Ascension I. (Br.) · St. Helena (Br.) · I. S. Thomé (Port.) · Annobon (Sp.) · Fernando Po · Principe · Aldabra (Br.) · Comoro Is. (Fr.) · Mauritius 1552

Cape Town to Southampton 5995 · Madeira 4700 · Tenerife 4470 · Ascension to St. Helena 703 · St. Helena to Cape Town 1700 · Lobito B. to Cape Town 1440 · Cape Town to Fremantle 4950 · Durban to Mauritius 1552 · To Mauritius 1447

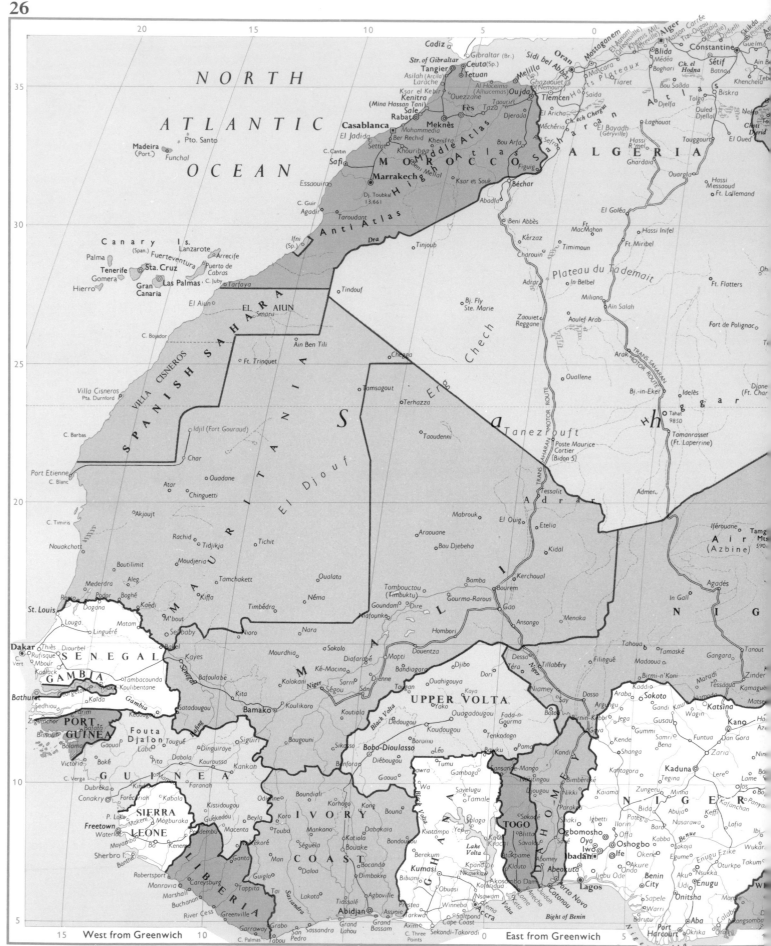

20 15 10 5 0

NORTH

ATLANTIC

OCEAN

35

Madeira
(Port.) Pto. Santo
Funchal

30

Canary Is.
(Span.) Lanzarote
Palma Fuerteventura Arrecife
Tenerife Sta. Cruz Puerto de
Gomera Gran C. Juby Cabras
Hierro Canaria Las Palmas C. Juby Tarfaya

C. Bojador

25

Villa Cisneros
Pta. Durnford

C. Barbas

20

C. Timiris
Port Étienne
C. Blanc

Cadiz
Str. of Gibraltar Gibraltar (Br.) Sidi bel Abbès Oran Mostaganem El Asnam Khemis Mil. Alger Constantine
Tangier Ceuta (Sp.) Melilla (Orléansville) Aumale Blida Sétif
Asilah (Arcila) Tetuan Al Hoceima Maison Carrée Tizi-Ouzou Khenchela
Larache (Alhucemas) Oujda Tiaret Boghari Ch. el Béjaïa
Ksar el Kebir Taourirt Tlemcen Haut Plateaux Saïda Hodna Biskra
Kenitra Fès Taza Djerada El Aricha Djelfa Ouled Chott
(Mina Hassan Tani) Meknès Mécheria Djellal El Oued
Salé Ksar es Souk El Bayadh Laghouat Touggourt Chott
Rabat Middle Atlas Bou Arfa (Géryville) Hassi Negrin Djerid
Casablanca Figuig R'mel Ghardaïa Ouargla
El Jadida Khouribga Béchar El Goléa Hassi Ft. Lallemand
C. Cantin Settat Beni Mellal Abadla Messaoud
Safi Marrakech Ksar es Souk Beni Abbès Ft. MacMahon Hassi Inifel
Essaouira Dj. Toubkal Kerzaz Ft. Miribel
C. Guir 13,661 Timimoun
Agadir Anti Atlas Dra Tinjoub Charouin Plateau du Tademait
Taroudant In-Belbel Ft. Flatters
Ifni (Sp.)
Tindouf Bj. Fly Adrar
Ste. Marie Aïn Salah
El Aiun Zaouiet Aoulef Arab
Smara Reggane Fort de Polignac

EL AAIUN Arak Bj.-in-Eker Idelès Djane
SPANISH SAHARA Chegga Ouallene (Ft. Char
Aïn Ben Tili Trans Saharan Motor Route
Ft. Trinquet Tamsagout Tahat Tamanrasset
VILLA CISNEROS Terhazza 9850 (Ft. Laperrine)
El Djouf Tanezrouft Admer
Idjil (Fort Gouraud) Taoudenni Poste Maurice
Char Cortier
Ouadane (Bidon 5) Tessalit
Atar Mabrouk El Ouig Iférouane Tamg
Chinguetti Araouane Etelia In Gall Air Mts
Rachid Bou Djebeha Kidal Agadés (Azbine) 590
Akjoujt Nouakchott Tidjikja Tichit
Boutilimit Moudjeria Tamchakett Oualata Kerchoual Menaka NIG
Mederdra Aleg Kiffa Néma Bamba Bourem
Podor Kaédi Timbédra Tombouctou Gourma-Rarous Gao
St. Louis Dagana Boghé M'bout Nara (Timbuktu) Tahoua Tamaské
Louga Matam Selibaby Nioro Goundam Diré Ansongo In Gall Gangara Tanout
Linguère MAURITANIA Niafounke Hombori Birni-n'Koni
Dakar Thiès Diourbel Bakel Kayes Mourdiah Sokolo Douentza Dessa Tillabéry Filingué Madaoua Maradi Zinder
Rufisque SENEGAL Diafarabé Mopti Djibo Téra Niamey Say Dosso Araba Gangara Kamague
Mbour GAMBIA Tambacounda Koulikoro Ké-Macina Bandiagara Ouahigouya Kaya Birni-Kebbi Gandi Matse
Bathurst Koulibantane Bafoulabé Kolokani Diénné Dori UPPER VOLTA Gusau Kano
PORT Banjul Kita MALI Ségou Sarrr Ouagadougou Yako Fada-n- Argungu Kaddi Gummi Samri Funtua Zaria
GUINEA Sedhiou Satadougou Bamako Koutiala San Gourma Jega Shanga Bena Kaduna
Bissau Fouta Kédougou Sikasso Koudougou Tenkodogo Botou Kende Kontagora Tegina
Bolama Djalon Tougué Siguiri Bougouni Bobo-Dioulasso Léo Bawku Kandi Zungeru Lere Lame
Victoria Labé Dabola Banfora Diébougou Boromo Pama Nikki Kaiama Minna
Boké GUINEA Pita Dinguiraye Tumu Gaoua Gambaga Natitingou Bimbéréké Bida
C. Verga Dubréka Faranah Kankan Wa Parakou Ilorin Lokoja
Conakry Forécariah Kabala Kissidougou Boundiali Kong Savelugu Diougou Shaki Oshogbo Akure
P. Loko Kindia Beyla Korhogo Bouna Tamale NIGERIA Igbetti Ile Okene
SIERRA Makeni Mgburaka Guékédou Odienné IVORY Bondoukou Salaga Yendi TOGO DAHOMEY Ogbomosho Iwo Ife
LEONE Freetown Moyamba Macenta Touba Katiola Kpandu Sokodé Abeokuta Ibadan Enugu Ezike
Waterloo Bo Kenema Séguéla Bouaké GHANA Blitta Porto Novo Benin
Sherbro I. Bonthe Pendembu COAST Bocanda Lake Nsawam Kloto Atakpame Lagos Benin City Enugu
Moyamba Ganta Man Bibiani Volta Kumasi Anecho Cotonou Sapele
LIBERIA Guiglo Daloa Dimbokro Obuasi Kpandu Akosombo Dam Ijebu Ode Warri Onitsha
Robertsport Tai Lakota Agboville Prestea Winneba Lomé Akure Port Aba
Monrovia Tappita Sassandra Accra Cape Coast Harcourt Okrika Calabar
Marshall River Cess Guiglo Grand Axim Sekondi-Takoradi Niger Delta
Buchanan Greenville Lahou C. Three Delta
Abidjan Grand Points
Careysburg Bassam
San Pedro Assinie

Tabou
Grabo Tabou
Garraway
C. Palmas

MOROCCO
High Atlas Sahara
ALGERIA
Hoggar
Adrar

Chech

Er
Tanezrouft

El Djouf

15 10 West from Greenwich 0 East from Greenwich 5

Bight of Benin

5

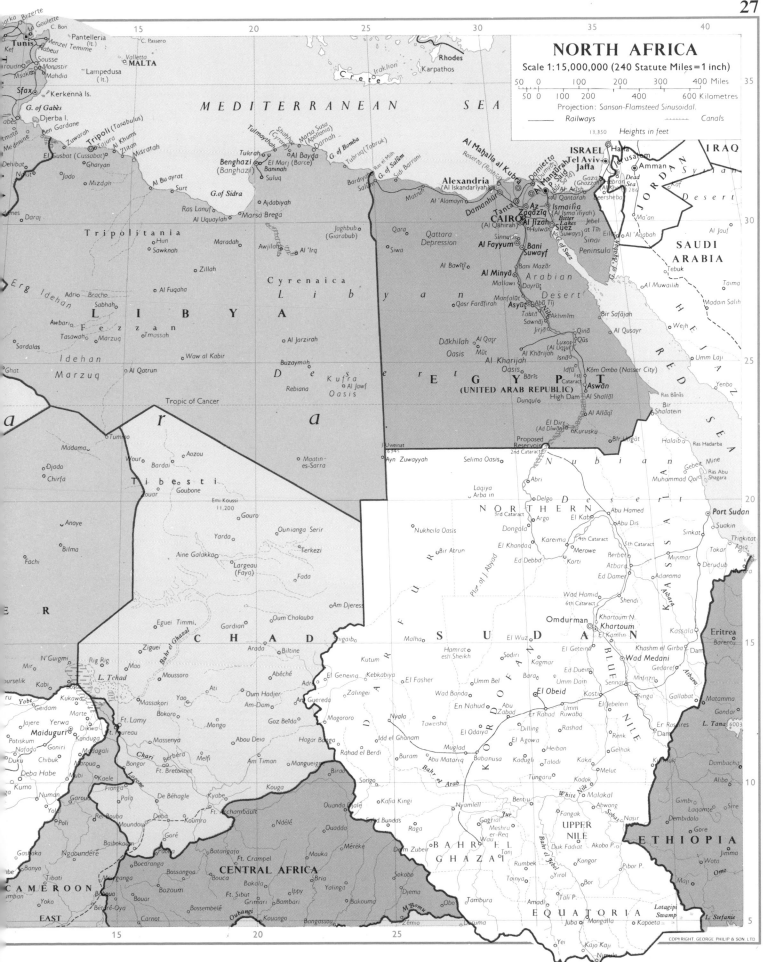

NORTH AFRICA
Scale 1:15,000,000 (240 Statute Miles=1 inch)

50 0   100   200   300   400 Miles
50 0 100 200   400   600 Kilometres

Projection: Sanson-Flamsteed Sinusoidal.
——— Railways   ·········· Canals
13,350   Heights in feet

MEDITERRANEAN SEA

Tunis
La Goulette
Bizerte
C. Bon
Pantelleria (It.)
Menzel Temime
Nabeul
Sousse
Monastir
Mahdia
Valletta MALTA
Lampedusa (It.)
Sfax
Kerkenna Is.
G. of Gabès
Djerba I.
Ben Gardane
Medenine
Dehibat

Rhodes
Crete Iraklion Karpathos

ISRAEL Haifa
Tel Aviv Jaffa Jerusalem
Gaza Dead Sea Amman
JORDAN
IRAQ
Syrian Desert

Zuwarah Tripoli (Tarabulus)
Tajura Al Khums
Zliten Misratah
El Gusbat (Cussabat)
Gharyan
Jado
Mizdah
Al Bu'ayrat
Surt

Tukrah (Teuchira)
Shahhat (Cyrene)
Al Bayda
Marsa Susa (Apollonia)
Darnah
G. of Bomba
Tubruq (Tobruk)
Ras el Milh
Bardiyah
Salum G. of Salum Sidi Barrani
Matruh Sidi Abd er Rahman

Alexandria (Al Iskandariyah)
Rosetta (Rashid)
Damietta Dumyat
Al Mansurah Port Said
Az Zaqaziq
Tanta Al Qantarah
Ismailia (Al Isma'iliyah)
CAIRO (Al Qahirah)
Al Jizah Hulwan
Suez Bitter Lakes
G. of Suez Jebel at Tih
Al 'Arish Beersheba
Nakhl Eilat Al 'Aqabah
SAUDI ARABIA
Tebuk
Al Muwailih
Madain Salih
Taima

Benghazi (Banghazi)
El Marj (Barce)
Baninah Suluq
Ajdabiyah
Ras Lanuf
Marsa Brega
Al Uquaylah

G. of Sidra

Tripolitania
Hun
Sawknah
Zillah

Cyrenaica

Al Fuqaha

Erg Idehan
Adrio Bracho
Sabhah
Awbari Fezzan
Tasawah
Marzuq
Tmassah
Waw al Kabir

Ghadames?
Sardalas

Idehan
Marzuq
Ghat
Al Qatrun

Jaghbub (Giarabub)
Maradah
Awjilah
Al 'Iraq

Qara
Siwa

Qattara Depression

Damanhur
Al Fayyum
Bani Suwayf
Al Minya
Al Bawiti
Mallawi
Bani Mazar
Dayrut

Arabian

Libyan

Desert

Dakhila Al Qasr
Dakhla Oasis Mut
Al Kharijah Oasis
Baris

Buzaymah
Rebiana
Kufra Al Jawf Oasis

Al Jarirah
Waw al Kabir

Maatin-es-Sarra

Tummo
Madama
Woour Bardai
Djado
Chirfa
Aozou
Anaye
Bilma
Fachi
Yarda
Goubone
Emi Koussi 11,200
Gouro
Ounianga Serir
Terkezi
Fada

Tibesti

S a h a r a

Desert

Tropic of Cancer

Qasr Farafirah
Asyut Abu Tij
Tahta Akhmim
Sawhaj
Jirja
Qina
Luxor (Al Uqsur)
Al Khârijah
Isna
Idfu
Kôm Ombo (Nasser City)
Aswan
High Dam Al Shallal
Dunqul
El Dirr (Ad Diwan) Kurusku
Proposed Reservoir
2nd Cataract
J. Uweinat 6,345
Ayn Zuwayyah
Selima Oasis

EGYPT
(UNITED ARAB REPUBLIC)

Al Qusayr
Bir Safajah

Bir Shalatein

RED SEA

HEJAZ

Umm Laji
Wejh
Yenbo

Ras Bânâs

Halaib Ras Hadarba
Gebel Mine
Muhammad Qol Ras Abu Shagara

Nubian Desert

Nukheila Oasis
Laqiya Arba'in
Abri
Delgo
NORTHERN
3rd Cataract
Dongala
Argo
El Khandaq
Kareima 4th Cataract
Merowe 5th Cataract
Korti
Ed Debba Berber
Atbara
Ed Dameir

Abu Hamed
El Kab
Abu Dis

Port Sudan
Suakin
Sinkat
Trinkitat Aqiq

Bir Atrun
Plat of J. Abyad

Tibu

Ounianga Kebir?
Largeau (Faya)

Am Djeress

N'Guigmi
Rig Rig
Mao
Ziguei Bahr el Ghazal
Eguei Timmi
Gardian

Moussoro

CHAD

Digaibo
Malha
Arada Biltine

Wad Hamid
Shendi
6th Cataract
Khartoum N.
Omdurman Khartoum
El Kamlin
El Wuz
El Geteina
Kassala

Khashm el Girba Dam
Gedaref
Gallabat

SUDAN

Eritrea
Barentu

Matamma

Gondar

Mir
ourselik Kabi
N'Djamena
Massakori Yao
Bokoro
Ft. Lamy
L. Tchad
Kukawa
Geidam
Marte
Dikwa
Yerwa Maiduguri
Konduga
Ft. Foureau

Ati
Oum Hadjer
Am-Dam
Abéché
Adré Abéché
Am Guereda
Goz Beida

Kutum
Kebkabiya
El Geneina
Zalingei

Hamrat esh Sheikh
Sodiri
Kagmar
Bara
Umm Dam

El Fasher
Mogororo

KORDOFAN

En Nahud
Umm Bel
Wad Banda
El Obeid
Abu Zabad
Er Rahad Umm Ruwaba

Ed Dueim
Kosti
El Jebelein

Sennar
Singa

Wad Medani

BLUE NILE

Er Roseires Dam
L. Tana 6003

Dambacha?

Aliba

Jajere Yerwa
Potiskum
Nafada
Duku
Goniri
Chibuk
Mdagali
Maroua
Deba Habe
Kaele
Kumo
Numan
Garoua

Massenya
Bongor Berberati?
Melfi
Chari
Ft. Bretonnet
Am Timan
Mangueigne

Fianga
Rei-Bouba
Baïbokoum

Birao

Sorigo

Tungaru

Kadugli
Talodi
Kaka
Heiban
El Agowa
Rashad

Dilling
Muglad
Abu Matariq
Babanusa
Kodok
Melut

Renk
Gelhak

Gallabat

Matammo

Gondar

DARFUR

Nyala
Taweisha
Idd el Ghanam
Buram

BAHR EL GHAZAI

Abou Deia
Hagar Banga
Rahad el Berdi

Kafia Kingi
Deim Zubeir
Raga

Nyamlell
Gogrial
Meshra er-Req
Wau
Tonj
Rumbek

Bahr el Arab
White Nile
Malakal
Abwong
Fangak Nasir
Bentiu

UPPER NILE

Sobat
Sire
Gimbi
Laqamte
Dembidola
Gore
Wota
Omo
Jimma

ETHIOPIA

CAMERON
EAST
Yoko
Banyo
Tibati
Ngaoundéré
Bocaranga
Bozoum
Bouar
Baoro
Bossembélé
Bossangoa
Bogangolo?

CENTRAL AFRICA
Ft. Sibut
Bria
Ippy
Bakala
Grimari
Bambari
Bakouma
Djema

Kouango
Bangassou

M'Bomu

Deim
Tambura
Amadi

Sokobo
Merèke
Mouka
Ouadda
Ouanda Djalle

Birao

Oubangi

Zemio L. Stefanie

EQUATORIA
Yei
Kajo Kaji
Nimule

Juba
Mongalla
Pibor P.
Kongor
Tali P.
Mali
Lotagipi Swamp
Kapoeta

Duk Fadiat
Akobo P.
Wota

COPYRIGHT GEORGE PHILIP & SON LTD

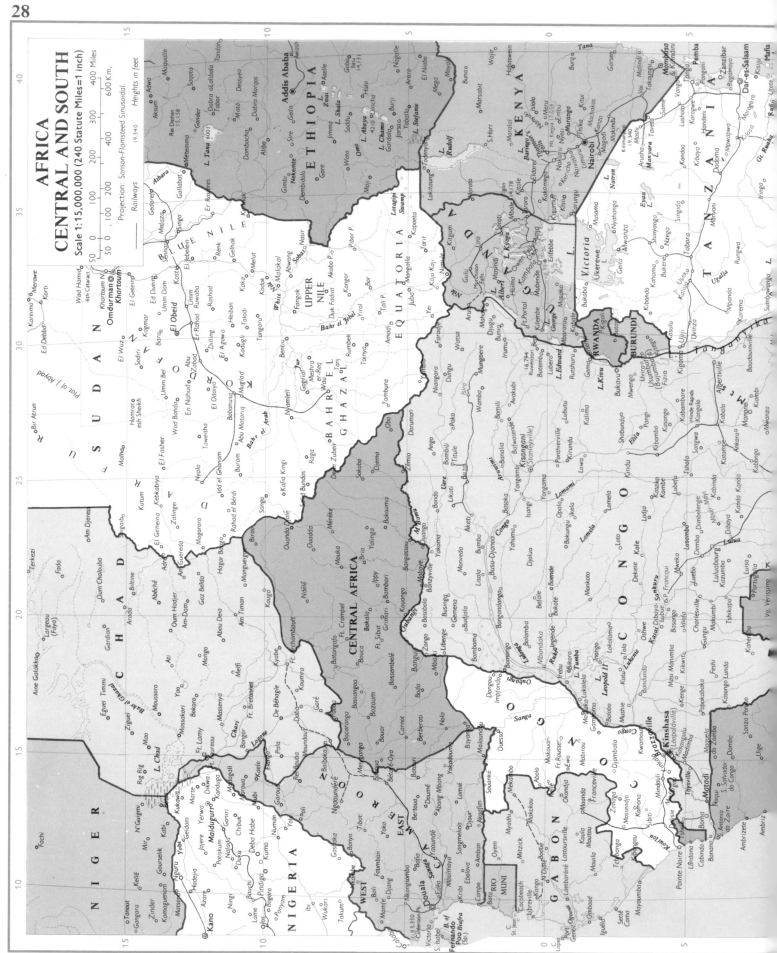

28

AFRICA
CENTRAL AND SOUTH
Scale 1:15,000,000 (240 Statute Miles=1 inch)

Projection: Sanson-Flamsteed Sinusoidal.

Railways

Heights in feet

50   0   .   100   200   300   400   Miles
50   0   100   200   300   400   600 Km.

19,340

N I G E R

C H A D

S U D A N

ETHIOPIA

Addis Ababa

KENYA

Nairobi

TANZANIA

Zanzibar
Dar-es-Salaam

NIGERIA

CAMEROON
WEST

EAST
CAMEROON

RIO
MUNI

GABON

CENTRAL AFRICA

CONGO

CONGO

Kinshasa
(Leopoldville)

Matadi

RWANDA
BURUNDI

UGANDA

BLUE NILE
WHITE NILE
UPPER NILE
EQUATORIA
BAHR EL GHAZAL
KORDOFAN

Khartoum
Omdurman

L. Victoria

L. Tanganyika

L. Albert
L. Edward
L. Kivu

SOUTH ATLANTIC OCEAN

INDIAN OCEAN

MALAGASY REPUBLIC

MALAGASY REPUBLIC

On same scale as General Map

ANGOLA

SOUTH WEST AFRICA

Ovamboland

Damaraland

Namaqualand

Great

Kalahari

BOTSWANA

RHODESIA

Salisbury

Bulawayo

MALAWI

MOZAMBIQUE

Lourenço Marques

SWAZILAND

TRANSVAAL

Pretoria

Johannesburg

ORANGE FREE STATE

Bloemfontein

LESOTHO

NATAL

Durban

REPUBLIC OF SOUTH AFRICA

CAPE PROVINCE

Cape Town

Port Elizabeth

East London

KATANGA

Luanshya

Kitwe

Lusaka

Z A M B I A

BAROTSELAND

Caprivi Strip

Windhoek

Walvis Bay

Lüderitz

East from Greenwich

COPYRIGHT. GEORGE PHILIP & SON, LTD.

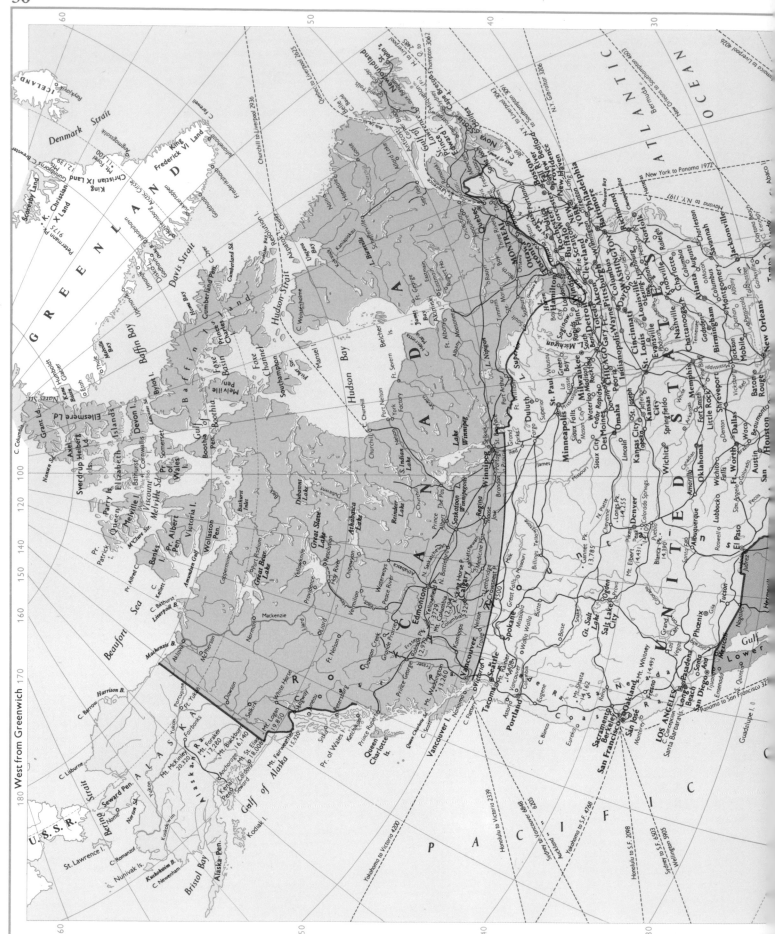

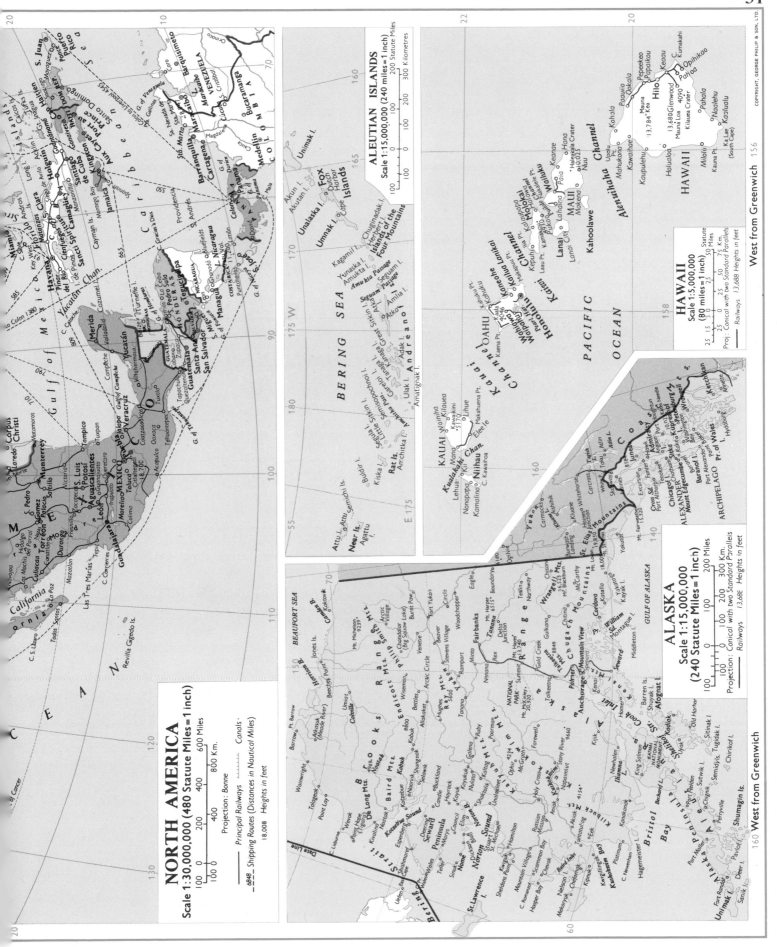

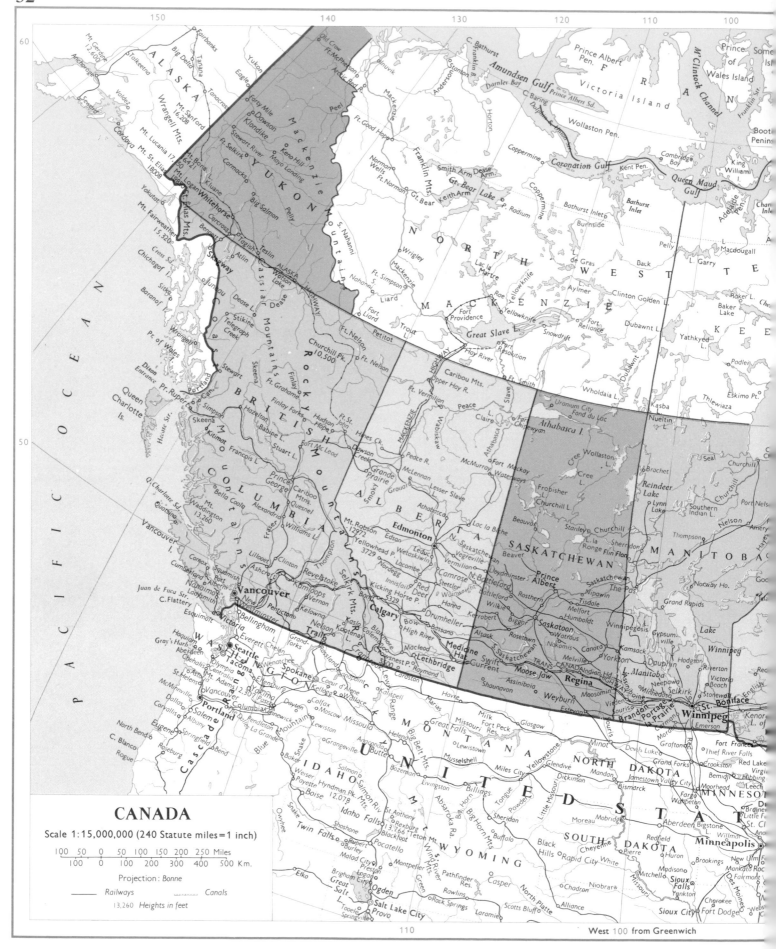

32

CANADA

Scale 1:15,000,000 (240 Statute miles=1 inch)

100 50 0 50 100 150 200 250 Miles
100 0 100 200 300 400 500 Km.

Projection: Bonne

Railways   Canals
13,260 Heights in feet

West 100 from Greenwich

33

GREENLAND

King Frederick VI Coast

Baffin Bay

Davis Strait

ATLANTIC

Hudson Strait

Hudson Bay

LABRADOR

NEWFOUNDLAND

St. John's

QUEBEC

Gulf of St. Lawrence

ONTARIO

NEW BRUNSWICK

NOVA SCOTIA

Halifax

MONTREAL

Quebec

OTTAWA

TORONTO

Lake Superior

Lake Huron

Lake Michigan

NEW YORK

BOSTON

NEW YORK

CHICAGO

DETROIT

Buffalo

MILWAUKEE

ATLANTIC OCEAN

COPYRIGHT GEORGE PHILIP & SON LTD.

95 90 85 80 75 70

ONTARIO

QUEBEC

NEW BRUNSWICK

Winnipeg
Lake of the Woods

MINNESOTA
Duluth

Lake Superior

MAINE

45

MONTREAL
Ottawa
Quebec

VERMONT
NEW HAMPSHIRE

WISCONSIN

Lake Michigan

Lake Huron

TORONTO

Buffalo

NEW YORK

MASS.
Boston
CONN.

Minneapolis
St. Paul

Milwaukee
Grand Rapids

Rochester
Syracuse
Albany

40

IOWA

Des Moines

CHICAGO

DETROIT
Cleveland
Akron

PENNSYLVANIA

NEW YORK

Philadelphia

OHIO

Pittsburgh

NEW JERSEY

Columbus
Cincinnati

WEST VIRGINIA

Baltimore
Washington D.C.
DEL.

Kansas City
St. Louis

Indianapolis

Richmond

35

MISSOURI

KENTUCKY

VIRGINIA

Louisville

Norfolk

Tulsa

Nashville
Memphis

NORTH CAROLINA

TENNESSEE

Charlotte

Raleigh

OKLAHOMA

ARKANSAS

Little Rock

Atlanta

SOUTH CAROLINA

Birmingham
MISSISSIPPI
ALABAMA

Charleston

GEORGIA

30

Dallas

Shreveport

Jackson

Montgomery
Columbus

Savannah

Houston

LOUISIANA
Baton Rouge

Mobile

Jacksonville

FLORIDA

New Orleans

Delta of the Mississippi

ATLANTIC OCEAN

Tampa
St. Petersburg

Bahama Islands

25

GULF OF MEXICO

Miami

Key West

Andros I.

95 Woot from Greenwich 90 85 80 75

COPYRIGHT. GEORGE PHILIP & SON. LTD.

WEST INDIES

Scale 1:12,000,000
(192 Statute Miles = 1 inch)

Projection: Bi-polar oblique
Conical Orthomorphic.

Railways
Canals
Heights in feet

BERMUDA
1:1,000,000
(16 m = 1 in)

St. George's
St. David's I.
Castle Harb.
Tucker's Town
Ireland I.
Somerset
Spanish Flatt
North Village Town
Hamilton

LEEWARD ISLANDS
1:8,000,000
(128 m = 1 in)

Anguilla
St. Martin (Fr.)
St. Maarten (Neth.)
Saba (Neth.)
St. Eustatius (Neth.)
St. Barthélemy (Fr.)
St. Christopher (St. Kitts)
Nevis
Redonda
Barbuda (Br.)
St. John's
Antigua
Montserrat (Br.)
Plymouth
Guadeloupe
Basse Terre
Marie-Galante (Fr.)
Grand Bourg
Dominica
Roseau

JAMAICA
1:8,000,000
(128 m = 1 in)

Montego Bay
Kingston
Spanish Town
Port Royal
Port Antonio
Port Morant
Portland Point

TRINIDAD & TOBAGO
1:8,000,000

Tobago
Port of Spain
Gulf of Paria
San Fernando
TRINIDAD

WINDWARD ISLANDS
1:8,000,000
(128 m = 1 in)

Martinique Passage
Fort de France
MARTINIQUE
St. Lucia Channel
Castries
St. Lucia
Soufrière
St. Vincent
Kingstown
St. Vincent Passage
Bequia
Canouan
Carriacou
Grenada
St. George's
The Grenadines

BARBADOS
Speightstown
Bridgetown

ATLANTIC OCEAN

BAHAMA ISLANDS (United Kingdom)
Little Abaco I.
Grand Bahama I.
Great Abaco I.
Nassau
New Providence I.
Eleuthera I.
Berry Is.
Andros Island
GREAT BAHAMA BANK
Cat I.
San Salvador or Watling's I.
Conception I.
Rum Cay
Long I.
Crooked I.
Acklins I.
Great Exuma I.
Mayaguana I.
Little Inagua I.
Great Inagua I.
Turks Is. (Br.)
Caicos Islands (Br.)

MIAMI
Fort Lauderdale
West Palm Beach
Fort Pierce
FLORIDA
U.S.A.
Fort Myers
Key West
Florida Keys
Dry Tortugas
GULF OF MEXICO

MEXICO
Yucatán Channel
Isla de Cozumel

C U B A
Havana
Matanzas
Cárdenas
Santa Clara
Cienfuegos
Sancti Spíritus
Camagüey
Holguín
Santiago de Cuba
Guantánamo
Pinar del Río
Isle of Pines (I. de Pinos)

JAMAICA
Montego Bay
Kingston
Spanish Town

HAITI
Port-au-Prince
Cap-Haïtien
Gonaïves
DOMINICAN REP.
Santo Domingo
Santiago
HISPANIOLA

PUERTO RICO (U.S.A.)
San Juan
Ponce
Mayagüez
Arecibo

Virgin Is.
GREATER ANTILLES
LESSER ANTILLES

CARIBBEAN SEA

Cayman Islands (Br.)
Grand Cayman

HONDURAS
Tegucigalpa
NICARAGUA
Managua
COSTA RICA
San José
PANAMA
CANAL ZONE
Colón
Panama
PACIFIC OCEAN

COLOMBIA
BARRANQUILLA
Cartagena
Santa Marta
Medellín

VENEZUELA
CARACAS
Maracaibo
MARACAIBO
Valencia
Barquisimeto
Gulf of Venezuela
Trinidad
Port of Spain
Orinoco
Ciudad Bolívar

Aruba (Neth.)
Curaçao (Neth.)
Bonaire (Neth.)

COPYRIGHT GEORGE PHILIP & SON, LTD.

West from Greenwich

SOUTH AMERICA

Scale 1 : 30,000,000 (480 Statute Miles = 1 inch)

100 0 100 200 300 400 500 600 Miles
100 0 200 400 600 800 Kilometres

Projection : Bonne

——— Railways   5034 ——— Shipping Routes
(Distances in Nautical Miles)

23,081 Heights in feet

COPYRIGHT GEORGE PHILIP & SON LTD.

AUSTRALIA

Scale 1:13,500,000 (216 Statute miles = 1 inch)

100 50 0   100   200   300 Miles
100 50 0   100   200   300   400
Km.

Projection : Bonne

——— Railways   ·3654 Heights in feet

I N 120 D O N E S I A

T I M O R   S E A

I N D I A N   O C E A N

Ashmore Is.

Cartier I.

Bonaparte

C. Londonderry
C. Talbot
C. Bougainville B.
Admiralty G.
Vansittart B.
Montague Sd.
York Sd.
Bruriswick B.
Collier B.
Leveque
King Sd.
Yampi Sound
King Leopold Ras.
Mt. Ord 3070
Glenroy
Meda
Derby
C. Baskerville
Carnot B.
C. Boileau
Broome
Fitzroy
Hall's Creek
Fitzroy Crossing
C. Latouche Treville
Dampier Downs
C. Bossut
La Grange

Mount Melville
P. Essington
Goulburn Is.
A. Junction B.
Van Diemen
Dundas Str.
C. Ford
Cockburn Sd.
Bathurst
Clarence Str.
P. Darwin
Darwin
Van Diemen Gulf
Castle

Pt. Blaze
Anson B.
C. Ford
Jos. Bonaparte Gulf
Cambridge G.
Queens Chan.
Wyndham
Gulf Basin
Kununurra
Victoria

Rum Jungle
Batchelor
Frances Creek
Pine Creek
Daly
Katherine
Roper
Mataranka
Larrimah
Victoria River Downs
Daly W.

Mt. Hann 2547

K i m b e r l e y

D'urack Range
Ord
Gordon Downs
Sturt

Newcastle Waters
Wave Hill
L. Woods
Puwe
Cree

N O R T H

T E R R I

The Granites
Hordern Hills 1600
Davenpo Ra.

Eighty Mile Beach
Port Site Three
Mount Goldsworthy
De Grey
Canning Basin

C a n n i n g   B a s i n

G r e a t   S a n d y   D e s e r t

Gregory Lake

L. Dora

L. Blanche

L. Mackay

L. Macdonald

Mt. Ziel 4955

Bar
Cre

R e y n o l d s   R a.

M a c d o n n e l l   R a.

Dampier Archipelago
P. Hedland
Hampton Har.
Dampier
Monte Bello Is.
Barrow I.
Cape Preston
Roebourne
Mimingarra
Shaw
Marble Bar
Throssell Ra.
Robertson Ras.
Mt. Nicholas

N.W. Cape
Exmouth
Learmonth
Pt. Cloates
Hamersley Home Sta.
Onslow
Mt. Enid
Mt. Brockman 3654
Mt. Bruce 4024
Ophthalmia Range
Fortescue Ra.
Hamersley Ra.
Wittenoom Gorge
Pilbara
Mt. Tom Price
Mount Whaleback
Ashburton

L. Disappointment

G i b s o n   D e s e r t

Rawlinson Ras.

Alic
Spr

James Ra.
Palmer
Finke
Hugh

C. Farquhar
C. Cuvier
Geographe Chan.
Bernier I.
Dorre I.
Naturaliste Chan.
Dirk
Hartog I.
S. Passage
Steep Pt.
North
Cornarvon
Barlee Ra.
Lyons
Mt. Augustus 3627
Mt. Egerton 3262
Peak Hill
Gascoyne
West
Wooramel
Robinson
Ras.
Murchison
Basin
Sanford
Mt. Hale 2400
Meekatharra
Nannine
Cue
Wiluna
L. Buchanan
L. Carnegie
L. Wells

W E S T E R N

A U S T R A L I A

Ayers Rock 2820
L. Amadeus

Musgrave Ranges
Mt. Woodroffe 4970
Hamc
Alt

S O U T H

Gantheaume B.
P. Gregory
Northampton
Champion B.
Geraldton
Dongara
L. Monger
L. Moore
Mullewa
Yalgoo
Mt. Magnet
L. Austin
Sandstone
Lawlers
Leonora
Laverton
L. Rason
Yeo L.
L. Maurice
Maralinga
Oldea
Tarc

Coastal
Jurien B.
Wedge I.
Plains
Basin
Bonnie Rock
Bencubbin
Bullfinch
Southern Cross
Kanowna
Kalgoorlie
Coolgardie
Boulder
L. Lefroy
L. Raeside
Malcolm
L. Carey
Menzies
L. Ballard
L. Minigwal
Premier Downs
Rawlinna
Forrest
Deakin
Zanthus
Eucla Basin
Nullarbor Plain
Hampton Ra.
L. Eve

L. Cowan
Norseman
L. Dundas
Pt. Dover
Eyre
Eucla
Head of Bight
C. Adieu
Fowlers B.
Penon

Midland Junction
Perth
Swan
Northam
York
Merredin
Kellerberrin
Beverley
Brookton
The Johnston Lakes
Newdegate

Rottnest
Fremantle
Pinjarra
Kwinana
Narrogin
Collie
Wagin
Nyabing
Ravensthorpe
Esperance
Rocky Pt.
Pt. Culver
C. Pasley
C. Arid
Archipelago of the Recherche
Great Australian Bight

Streaky B.
C. Radstock
Anxie
Investigator G
Coffin B
Whi

Bunbury
Geographe B.
C. Naturaliste
Busselton
Augusta
C. Leeuwin
Collie
Katanning
Bridgetown
Manjimup
Pemberton
Gnowangerup
Hopetoun
Doubtful I. B.
Stirling Ra.
Barker
Mt. Barker
Albany
Pt. Hood
Esperance B.
le Grand
C. Knob

Flinders B.
Pt. d'Entrecasteaux
Pt. Nuyts
Denmark
Tor B.
King George Sound

Torres Strait

PAPUA

CORAL

SEA

D'Entrecasteaux Is.
Normanby I.

Solomon Is.
(Br.)

Guadalcanal

Rendova I.
Vangunu
Russell Is.
Santa Isabel
Misima I.
Rossel I.
Tagula I.
Louisiade Arch.
Bellona I.

Thursday I.
Banks I.
Prince of Wales I.
C. York
Newcastle B.
Endeavour Str.

Cloudy B.
Table B.
Orangerie B.
Samarai
East C.
Samarai
Vogel
D'Entrecasteaux Is.

C. Wessel
English Co. Is.
Elcho
C. Wilberforce
Melville B.
Gove
C. Arnhem
P. Bradshaw
Caledon B.
Arnhem B.
C. Grey
Blue Mud B.

Gulf of

Duifken Pt.
Albatross B.
Weipa
P. Musgrave
Wenlock
C. Grenville
Temple B.
Shelburne B.
C. Weymouth
Pt. Direction

Alyangula
Groote Eylandt
C. Beatrice
Limmen Bight
Maria I.

Carpentaria

Sir Edward Pellew Grp.
Vanderlin I.

Archer
Peninsula
Coen
Princess Charlotte B.
Bathurst B.
C. Melville

Cape
York
Mellwraith Ra.
Holroyd

Coleman

C. Keerweer

McArthur
Borroloola

Mornington I.
C. van Diemen
Wellesley Is.
Bentinck I.

C. Flattery
C. Bedford
Cooktown
C. Tribulation
Trinity B.
Mossman
Trinity B.

Osprey Rf.

Diane Bank

Willis Group

Coringa Is.

Lihou Rfs. & Cays.

Bellona I.

Barkly Tableland
L. Sylvester

Avon Downs

Normanby R.
Laura
Chillagoe
Mareeba
Atherton
Cairns
Innisfail
Ravenshoe
Bartle Frere 5287

Burketown
Croydon
Georgetown
Einasleigh
Forsayth
Normanton
Newcastle Ra.

Hinchinbrook I.
Ingham
Palm Is.
Halifax B.
Townsville

Flinders Rfs.

Camooweal
Dobbyn
Gregory Ra.
Norman

Seaview Ra.
C. Cleveland
C. Bowling Green
C. Upstart
Ayr
Home Hill
Bowen

Whitsunday I.
Cumberland Is.
Repulse B.

Swain Rfs.

Saumarez Rf.

Austral Downs
Mount Isa
Mary Kathleen
Cloncurry
Richmond
Hughenden
Pentland
Charters Towers
Collinsville
Netherdale
Mackay
C. Palmerston

Townshend I.
Townshend I.

Bird I.

Bellona Rfs.

Chesterfield Is.
(Fr.)

Duchess
Dajarra
Selwyn Range
Selwyn
Leichhardt

QUEENSLAND

Winton
Muttaburra

Belyando
Denham Ra.
Clermont
Aramac
Drummond Ra.
Isaacs R.
Mt. Morgan
Broadsound Ra.
Broad Sd.
Yeppoon
Rockhampton
Keppel B.

Georgina
Hay
Boulia

Longreach
Ilfracombe
Barcaldine
Alpha
Springsure
Emerald
C. Capricorn
Curtis
Curtis I.
Bustard Head

Simpson
Desert

Eyre Cr.
L. Machattie
Jundah
Barcoo
Yaraka
Blackall
Warrego Ra.
Expedition Ra.
Dawson R.
Theodore
Monto
Gladstone
Boyne
Biloela

Tropic of Capricorn

Charlotte Waters
Birdsville
Windorah

Mt. Acland 3200

Taroom
Wandoan
Burnett R.
Bundaberg
Hervey Bay
Sandy C.
Childers

TASMAN

Au
Macumba
L. Yamma Yamma

Cooper Creek

Adavale
Augathella
Chinchilla
Wandoan
Murgon
Wondai
Gayndah
Gympie
Maryborough
Nambour
Nanango
Fraser I.

Hanson
Macfarlane
Denison Ra.
Warburton

B
Strzelecki Cr.
Quilpie
Charleville
Mitchell
Roma
Kingaroy
Dalby
Moreton B.
Bribie I.
Moreton I.

SEA

L. Eyre North 52

L. Gregory
Thargomindah
Cunnamulla
Moonie
St. George
Toowoomba
Ipswich
Southport
Stradbroke
South Coast
Brisbane

AUSTRALIA
Stuart Ra.
L. Eyre South
L. Blanche
L. Callabonna

Dirranbandi
Goondiwindi
Warwick
Stanthorpe
Murwillumbah
Pt. Danger

Leigh Creek
Copley
Paroo
Paroo Chan.
Bourke
Barwon
Mungindi
Moree
Inverell
Tenterfield
Casino
Lismore
C. Byron
Ballina

New England Range
Glen Innes
Grafton
Clarence

Pimba
L. Frome
Wilcannia
Cobar
Walgett
Narrabri
Gwydir
Macleay

Mt. Barney 4449
Coffs Harbour

Woomera
Flinders Ranges
Broken Hill
Darling
Nyngan
Coonamble
Gunnedah
Liverpool Plains
Tamworth
Armidale
55.30
Round Mt.
Macleay

Gairdner
St. Mary's Pk. 3822
Hawker
Quorn
Main Barrier Ra.
Cadium
Hill
Menindee
Ivanhoe
Narromine
Dubbo
Gilgandra
Orange
Mudgee
Muswellbrook
Singleton
Kempsey
Taree
Pt. Macquarie

Eyre Penin.
Whyalla
Iron Knob
Port Pirie
Jamestown
Peterborough
Burra
Roto
Condobolin
Parkes
Forbes
Bathurst
Cessnock
Maitland
Sugarloaf Pt.
P. Stephens
Newcastle

NEW SOUTH WALES

Kimba
Cowell
Wallaroo
Kadina
Clare
Renmark
Wentworth
Mildura
Balranald
Hay
Hillston
Lake Cargelligo
Cootamundra
Young
Cowra
Lithgow
Penrith
Katoomba
Hawkesbury R.
SYDNEY
& Port Jackson

P. Lincoln
C. Catastrophe
Spencer Gulf
Yorke Penin.
Port Augusta
Murray River
Swan Hill
Kerang
Deniliquin
Wagga Wagga
Griffith
Murrumbidgee Irrigation Area
Narrandera
Leeton
Junee
Bowral
Wollongong
Shellharbour

Kangaroo I.
Spencer
Victor Harbor
Gulf St. Vincent
Adelaide
Pinnaroo
Ouyen
Balranald
Riverina
Murrumbidgee
Cootamundra
Yass
Goulburn
Nowra
Jervis B.

Backstairs Pass.
Encounter B.
Murray Bridge
Alexandrina
The Coorong
Mannum
Bordertown
Mallee
Kerang
Echuca
Tangamalanga
CAP. TERR.
Canberra
Queanbeyan
Batemans B.

Investigator Str.
Kingston S.E.
Naracoorte
Horsham
Wimmera
Swan Hill
Shepparton
Benalla
65.16
Mt. Bogong
Eucumbene
Cooma
Bega

Millicent
Mt. Gambier
Penola
Hamilton
Ararat
Maryborough
Castlemaine
Bendigo
Wangaratta
Mt. Kosciusko 7316
Bombala
Twofold B.

C. Northumberland
Discovery B.
Bridgewater
Portland
Port Fairy
Warrnambool
Colac
C. Otway
Ballarat
MELBOURNE
Gippsland
Moe
Morwell
Traralgon
Sale
Bairnsdale
Orbost
C. Howe
Mallacoota Inlet
Geelong
Port Phillip
Western
Wonthaggi
Ninety Mile Beach
Corner Inlet
Wilsons Promontory
Snowy

VICTORIA

Australian Alps

Ararat
Hamilton
Castlemaine
Australian Alps
Bombala
Ballarat
MELBOURNE
Geelong
C. Colac
C. Otway
Warrnambool
Port Fairy
Port Phillip
Phillip I.
Wonthaggi
Morwell
Traralgon
Moe
Sale
Yallourn
Bairnsdale
Orbost
Gippsland
C. Everard
Corner Inlet
Wilsons Promontory
Ninety Mile Beach
Snowy

King I.

Bass Strait

Hunter I.
C. Grim
Furneaux Group
Flinders I.
Cape Barren I.
C. Portland
Clarke I.

Sandy C.
Stanley
Burnie
Devonport
Ulverstone
Beaconsfield
Launceston
Scottsdale
St. Marys
Zeehan
380.9 Mt. Ossa
Great L.
Legges Tor 5160
Freycinet Penin.
Strahan
Queenstown
Macquarie Harb.

Low Rocky Pt.
Hobart
Mt. Field
New Norfolk
Tasman Penin.
St. Arthur
P. Davey
Bruny I.
Storm B.
S.E. Cape

TASMANIA
on same scale

140 145 150 155

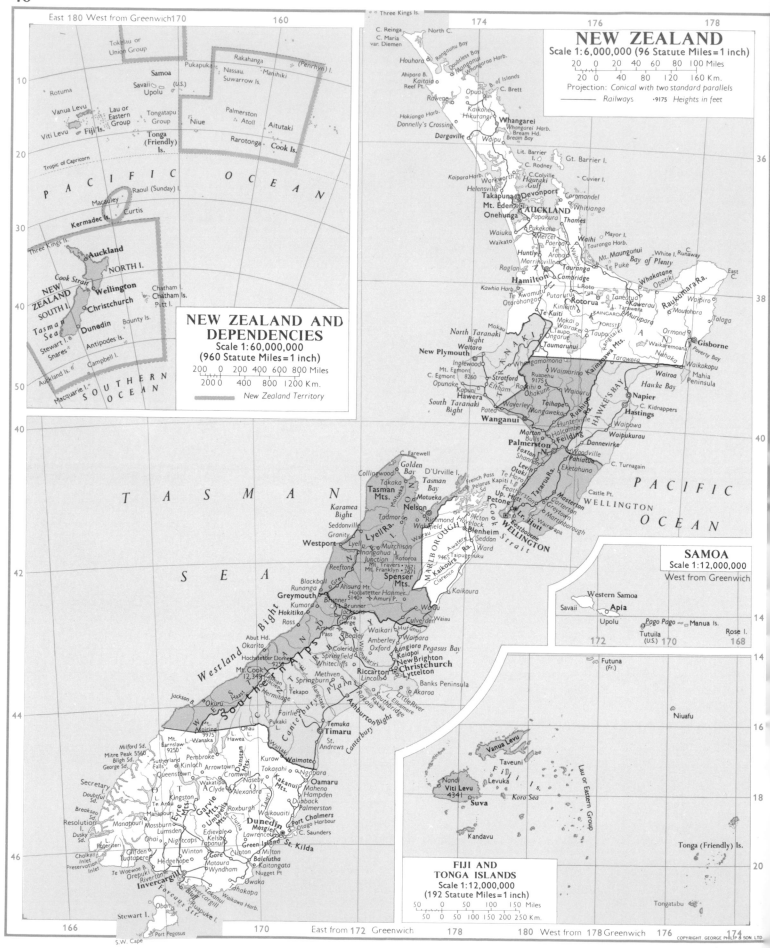

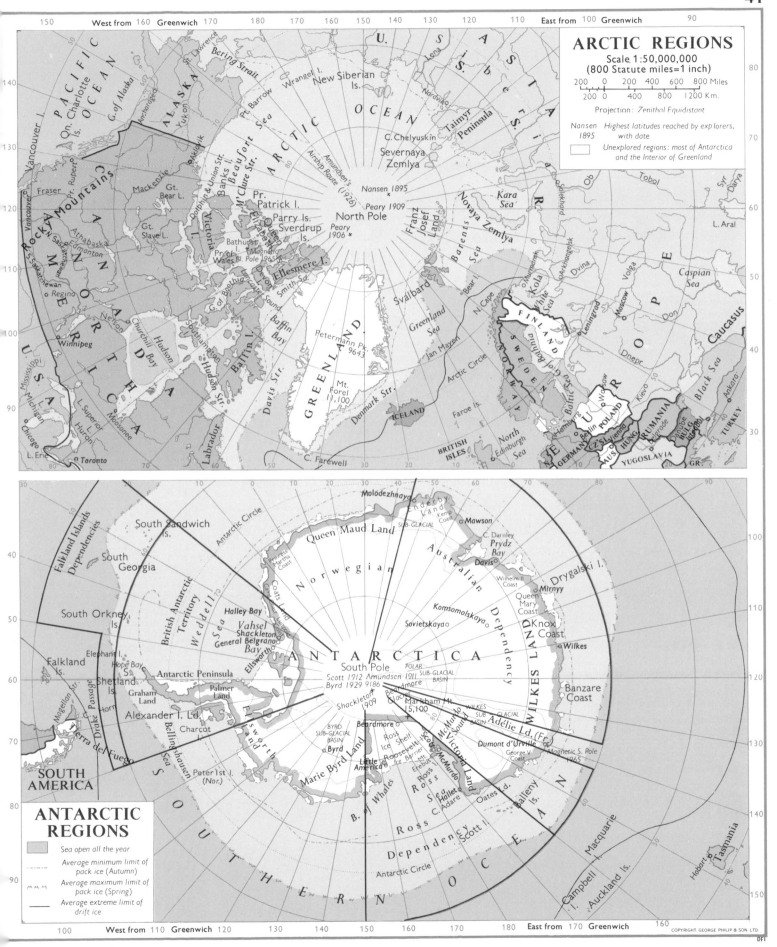

ARCTIC REGIONS
Scale 1:50,000,000
(800 Statute miles=1 inch)

200   0   200   400   600   800 Miles
200 0   400   800   1200 Km.

Projection: *Zenithal Equidistant*

Nansen   Highest latitudes reached by explorers,
1895   with date

Unexplored regions: most of Antarctica
and the Interior of Greenland

West from 160 *Greenwich* 170   180   170   160   150   140   130   120   110 *East from* 100 *Greenwich*   90

U. S. S. R.
ASIA
PACIFIC OCEAN
ARCTIC OCEAN
ALASKA
Yukon
Bering Strait
New Siberian Is.
Wrangel I.
Pt. Barrow
C. Chelyuskin
Taimyr Peninsula
Severnaya Zemlya
Airship Route (1926)
Amundsen's
Nansen 1895
North Pole
Peary 1909
Peary 1906
Franz Josef Land
Novaya Zemlya
Kara Sea
Barents Sea
Svalbard
Greenland Sea
Jan Mayen
Bear I.
N. Cape
Murmansk
Kola
White Sea
Arkhangelsk
Dvina
Volga
Moscow
Leningrad
Caspian Sea
L. Aral
Caucasus
GREENLAND
Petermann Pk. 9643
Mt. Forel 11,100
Denmark Str.
ICELAND
Faroe Is.
Arctic Circle
FINLAND
SWEDEN
NORWAY
Baltic
POLAND
GERMANY
NE
CZ'SL
AUS HUNG
RUMANIA
BULG
YUGOSLAVIA
GR.
TURKEY
Black Sea
Ankara
Danube
Belgrade
Kiev
Dnepr
Don
Warsaw
Berlin
Hamburg
Vienna
North Sea
Edinburgh
BRITISH ISLES
C. Farewell
Labrador
Davis Str.
Baffin Bay
Baffin I.
Hudson Str.
Southampton
Hudson Bay
Moosonee
Churchill
Nelson
Winnipeg
L. Superior
L. Huron
L. Michigan
L. Erie
Chicago
Toronto
Regina
Saskatchewan
Edmonton
Athabaska
Gt. Slave L.
Gt. Bear L.
Mackenzie
Coppermine
Victoria I.
Banks I.
Beaufort Sea
M'Clure Str.
Dolphin & Union Str.
Pr. Patrick I.
Parry Is.
Sverdrup Is.
Queen Elizabeth Is.
Bathurst
Pr. of Wales I.
Magnetic N. Pole 1965
Ellesmere I.
Devon I.
Lancaster Sound
Smith Sd.
G. of Boothia
ROCKY MOUNTAINS
NORTH AMERICA
U.S.A.
Mississippi
Fraser
Vancouver I.
Qn. Charlotte Is.
Pr. Rupert
G. of Alaska
Anchorage
Oakluk
St. Lawrence I.
Nordvik
Lena
Ob
Tobol
Syr Darya
Irtysh
Yenisey R.
Selekhard
EUROPE

ANTARCTIC REGIONS

Sea open all the year

Average minimum limit of
pack ice (Autumn)

Average maximum limit of
pack ice (Spring)

Average extreme limit of
drift ice

West from 110 *Greenwich* 120   130   140   150   160   180 *East from* 170 *Greenwich* 160

ANTARCTICA
South Pole
Scott 1912 Amundsen 1911
Byrd 1929 9186
Queen Maud Land
Norwegian
Enderby Land
Kemp Coast
Mawson
SUB GLACIAL
C. Darnley
Prydz Bay
Davis
Princess Martha Coast
Coats Land
Wilhelm II Coast
Drygalski I.
Mirnyy
Queen Mary Coast
Komsomolskaya
Sovietskaya
Australian Dependency
Knox Coast
Wilkes
WILKES LAND
Banzare Coast
POLAR SUB-GLACIAL BASIN
Amore
Markham Mt. 15,100
WILKES SUB GLACIAL
Adélie Ld. (Fr.)
Dumont d'Urville
George V Coast
Magnetic S. Pole 1965
Victoria Land
McMurdo Sound
Scott McMurdo
Ross Sea
Mt. Erebus
Ross
Little America
Roosevelt I.
Ross Ice Shelf
The Barrier
B. of Whales
Ross Dependency
Antarctic Circle
Halley Bay
Vahsel
Shackleton
General Belgrano
Bay
Weddell Sea
British Antarctic Territory
South Orkney Is.
South Georgia
South Sandwich Is.
Falkland Islands Dependencies
Antarctic Circle
Molodezhnaya
Byrd
BYRD SUB-GLACIAL BASIN
Marie Byrd Land
Beardmore
Beard. Glac.
Shackleton 1909
Ellsworth Land
Bellingshausen Sea
Charcot
Alexander I. Ld.
Palmer Land
Graham Land
Antarctic Peninsula
Shetland Is.
Elephant I.
Hope Bay
Horn
Drake Passage
Magellan Str.
Terra del Fuego
SOUTH AMERICA
Falkland Is.
Peter 1st I. (Nor.)
SOUTHERN OCEAN
Oates Ld.
C. Adare
Hallett
Scott I.
Balleny Is.
Macquarie I.
Campbell I.
Auckland Is.
Tasmania
Hobart

ABBREVIATIONS

Afghan. – *Afghanistan*
Afr. – *Africa*
Alas. – *Alaska*
Alg. – *Algeria*
Amer. – *America*
Ant. – *Antarctica*
Arch. – *Archipelago*
Arg. – *Argentina*
A.S.S.R. – *Autonomous Soviet Socialist Republic*
Austral. – *Australia*
B. – *Bay, Bight (Baie, Bahia, Baia)*
Belg. – *Belgium*
Br., Brit. – *British, Britain*
C. – *Cape (Cabo), Coast*
co. – *County*
Cz. – *Czechoslovakia*
Den. – *Denmark*
Dept. – *Département, Department*
Dist. – *District*
Eng. – *England*
Fd. – *Fiord, Fjord*
Fin. – *Finland*
Fr. – *France*
Ger. – *Germany*
Gr. – *Greece*
Gt. – *Great*
Hung. – *Hungary*
I(s.) – *Island(s) (Isle, Île)*
Indon. – *Indonesia*
Ire. – *Ireland*
L. – *Lake, Lough, Loch, Lago*
Mor. – *Morocco*
Mozam. – *Mozambique*
Mts. – *Mountains, Monts.*
N. – *North, Northern*
Neth. – *Netherlands*
N.Z. – *New Zealand*
Nor. – *Norway*
Oc. – *Ocean*
Pac. – *Pacific*
Pen. – *Peninsula*
Phil. – *Philippines*
Pol. – *Poland*
Port. – *Portugal, Portuguese*
Prov. – *Province*
Pt. – *Point, Port*
Pto. – *Porto, Puerto (Port)*
R. – *River, Rio*
Reg. – *Region*
Rep. – *Republic*
R.S.F.S.R. – *Russian Soviet Federal Socialist Republic*
Rum. – *Rumania*
S. – *Sea, South*
S. Afr. – *Rep. of South Africa*
Scot. – *Scotland*
Si. Arab. – *Saudi Arabia*
S.S.R. – *Soviet Socialist Republic*
st. – *State*
St. – *Saint*
Str. – *Strait*
Swed. – *Sweden*
Switz. – *Switzerland*
Tanz. – *Tanzania*
Terr. – *Territory*
tn. – *Town*
U.S.A. – *United States of America*
U.S.S.R. – *Union of Soviet Socialist Republics*
Ven. – *Venezuela*
vol. – *Volcano*
W. – *West, Wadi, Wady*
Y. Slav. – *Yugoslavia*

The latitudes and longitudes given below are primarily intended as a guide to finding the places on the map, and in some cases are only approximate.

Congo denotes the former Belgian Congo: Congo (Fr.) the Republic of Congo formerly a part of French Equatorial Africa.

Map

A

9 Aachen, Germany ....50 47N 6 4 E
26 Aba, Nigeria.......... 5 10N 7 19 E
18 Abadan, Iran..........30 22N 48 20 E
7 Abbeville, France .....50 6N 1 50 E
13 Åbenrå, Denmark.....55 4N 9 26 E
4 Aberdare, Wales......51 43N 3 27W
5 Aberdeen, Scotland ...57 9N 2 6W
5 Aberdeen, co., Scotland57 18N 2 30W
4 Aberystwyth, Wales...52 25N 4 6W
26 Abidjan, Ivory Coast... 5 16N 3 58W
4 Abingdon, England 51 40N 1 17W
10 Abruzzi, Reg. Italy ....42 15N 14 0 E
18 Abu Dhabi,
Trucial Oman.......24 28N 54 23 E
26 Accra, Ghana 5 35N 0 15W
6 Achill, I., Ireland 53 58N 10 5W
18 Ad Dammān,
Si. Arabia ....26 22N 50 2 E
18 Ad Dawhah, Qatar ....25 19N 51 30 E
16 Adana, Turkey ....37 0N 35 16 E
18 Addis Ababa, Ethiopia . 9 2N 38 42 E
39 Adelaide, Australia ....34 55S 138 32 E
18 Aden, South Yemen ...12 50N 45 0 E
18 Aden, Gulf of, Asia ...13 0N 50 0 E
10 Adriatic Sea, Europe...43 0N 16 0 E
11 Ægean Sea, Europe....37 0N 25 0 E
16 Afghanistan, St., Asia ..33 0N 65 0 E
1 Africa, Continent .....11 0N 20 0 E
26 Agadés, Niger ....16 58N 8 10 E
19 Agra, India ....27 17N 78 13 E
37 Aguadas, Colombia 5 40N 75 38W
31 Aguascalientes, tn. & st.,
Mexico 22 0N 102 12W
19 Ahmadabad, India .....23 0N 72 40 E
13 Ahvenanmaa, I. Fin. ...60 15N 20 0 E
5 Airdrie, Scotland......55 53N 3 57W
7 Aix, France...........43 32N 5 27 E
7 Ajaccio, Corsica, Fr. ...41 55N 8 40 E
19 Ajmer, India..........26 28N 74 37 E
21 Akita, Japan ....39 45N 140 0 E
17 Akko (Acre), Israel ....32 35N 35 4 E
12 Akranes, Iceland 64 18N 21 53W
35 Akron, U.S.A. 41 7N 81 31W
14 Aktyubinsk, U.S.S.R. ..50 20N 57 0 E
12 Akureyria, Iceland.....65 37N 18 3W
19 Akyab, Burma ....20 15N 93 0 E
18 Al Aqabah, Jordan ....29 37N 35 0 E
18 Al Basrah, Iraq........30 30N 47 47 E
27 Al Bayda, Libya ....32 30N 21 30 E
27 Al Fayyum, Egypt .....29 17N 30 50 E
18 Al Hauta (Al Qatan),
S. Yemen...........15 55N 48 32 E
18 Al Hawra, S. Yemen ...15 45N 48 20 E
27 Al Jizah, Egypt........30 5N 31 10 E
18 Al Jazir,
Muscat & Oman.....18 33N 56 33 E
27 Al Khums, Libya ......32 30N 12 50 E
18 Al Kuwait, Kuwait ....29 28N 48 0 E
27 Al Mahalla al Kubra,
Egypt...............31 10N 31 0 E
27 Al Mansūrah, Egypt ...31 5N 31 25 E
16 Al Mawsil, Iraq ....36 30N 43 8 E
27 Al Minyā, Egypt.......28 7N 33 33 E
27 Al Qusayr, Egypt......26 14N 34 9 E
35 Alabama, st., U.S.A. ...33 0N 86 30W
37 Alagoinhas, Brazil 12 0S 38 20W
36 Alajuela, Costa Rica ...10 2N 84 8W
30 Alaska, st., U.S.A. 65 0N 150 0W
31 Alaska, Gulf of, ...58 0N 145 0W
32 Alaska Highway, Alaska62 30N 141 0W
11 Alba-Iulia, Rumania....46 8N 23 39 E
8 Albacete, Spain 39 0N 1 50W
11 Albania, Rep., Europe..41 0N 20 0 E
35 Albany, U.S.A.........42 40N 73 47W
28 Albert, L., E. Africa ... 1 30N 31 0 E
32 Alberta, Prov., Canada.54 40N 115 0W
28 Albertville, Congo .... 5 55S 29 9 E
13 Alborg, Denmark .....57 3N 9 52 E
34 Albuquerque, U.S.A. ..35 0N 106 40W
25 Aldabra, Is.,
Indian Ocean .... 9 22S 46 28 E
7 Alderney, I., Br. Isles ..49 42N 2 12W
4 Aldershot, England 51 15N 0 43W
10 Alessandria, Italy......44 54N 8 37 E
13 Alesund, Norway .....62 28N 6 5 E
31 Aleutian Is., Pac. Oc. ..50 0N 175 0W
31 Aleutian Ra., Alaska ...58 0N 135 0W
31 Alexander Arch., Alas .57 0N 135 0W
41 Alexander I., Ant.......69 0S 70 0W
27 Alexandria, Egypt .....31 10N 29 55 E
11 Alexandroupolis, Gr. ..40 50N 25 54 E
4 Alfreton, England 53 6N 1 22W
8 Algarve, Prov., Port. ..64 29N 22 10W
8 Algeciras, Spain ....36 9N 5 28 E
26 Alger, Algeria ....36 42N 3 8 E
26 Algeria, st., N. Afr.....32 50N 3 0 E
8 Alicante, Spain........38 23N 0 30W
38 Alice Springs, Austràl. .23 36S 133 53 E
19 Aligarh, India.........27 55N 78 10 E
19 Allahabad, India.......25 25N 81 58 E
6 Allen, Bog of, Ireland ..53 15N 7 0W
35 Allentown, U.S.A......40 36N 75 30W
14 Alma Ata, U.S.S.R. ....43 20N 76 50 E
8 Almeria, Spain 36 52N 2 32W
22 Alor Star, Malaya ..... 6 7N 100 22 E
10 Alps, Mts., Europe ....46 30N 8 0 E
7 Alsace, Prov., France ..48 15N 7 25 E
8 Alto-Alentejo, Prov.,
Portugal 38 55N 7 40W
9 Altona, Germany......53 32N 9 56 E
21 Amagasaki, Japan......34 48N 135 35 E
21 Amakusa, I., Japan.....32 15N 130 10 E
13 Amal, Sweden ....59 2N 12 40 E
34 Amarillo, U.S.A. 35 14N 101 46W
37 Amazon, R., S. Amer... 2 0S 53 30W
37 Amazonas, st., Brazil .. 4 20S 46 0W
23 Ambeno, Port. Timor.. 9 20S 124 30 E
29 Ambriz, Angola .... 7 48S 13 8 E
14 Amderma, U.S.S.R ....69 45N 61 30 E
7 Amiens, France ....49 54N 2 16 E
18 Amman, Jordan ....32 0N 35 52 E
20 Amoy, China ....24 30N 118 5 E
19 Amritsar, India ....31 35N 74 57 E
7 Amsterdam, Neth. ....52 23N 4 45 E
32 Amundsen Gulf, Can. .70 30N 123 0W
18 An Nafud, desert,
Si.Arabia ....28 15N 41 0 E
15 Anadyr, Gulf of,
U.S.S.R ....64 0N 180 0 E
31 Anchorage, Alaska 61 32N 149 50W
10 Ancona, Italy ....43 37N 13 30 E
8 Andalusia, Prov., Sp....37 35N 5 0W
16 Andaman Is., India.....12 30N 92 30 E
14 Andizhan, U.S.S.R. ....41 10N 72 0 E
37 Andes, Mts., S. Amer. . 7 0S 85 0W
19 Andhra Pradesh, st.,
India...............15 0N 80 0 E
31 Andreanof, Is.,
Aleutian Is..........51 0N 178 0W
8 Andorra, st., Europe ..42 30N 1 30 E
10 Andria, Italy..........41 13N 16 17 E
11 Andros, I., Greece ....37 50N 24 58 E
36 Andros I. Bahama Is....24 30N 78 0W
15 Angarsk, U.S.S.R. ....52 30N 104 0 E
7 Angers, France........47 30N 0 35W
4 Anglesey, co., Wales ..53 17N 4 20W
28 Angola, Port. Terr.,
Africa..............12 0S 18 0 E
7 Angoulême, France ....45 39N 0 10 E
7 Angoumois, Prov.,
France ....45 30N 0 25 E
5 Angus, co., Scotland ...56 45N 2 55W
20 Anhwei, Prov., China ..31 30N 117 30 E
7 Anjou, Prov., France...47 20N 0 30W
21 Anju, N. Korea ....39 30N 125 30 E
2 Ankara, Turkey ....40 0N 32 54 E
20 Anking, China ....30 32N 117 10 E
26 Annaba, Algeria.......36 55N 7 45 E
25 Annobon, I.,
G. of Guinea .... 1 35S 5 35 E
20 Anshan, China ....41 10N 123 0 E
21 Ansong, South Korea ..36 80N 127 30 E
41 Antarctica, Cont. 90 0S
7 Antibes, France ....43 34N 7 6 E
36 Antigua, I., W. Indies ..17 0N 61 50W
37 Antofagasta, Chile 23 50S 70 20W
6 Antrim & co., N. Ire. ..54 58N 6 20W
20 Antung, China ....40 10N 124 20 E
7 Antwerpen, Belgium ..51 13N 4 25 E
21 Aomori, Japan ....40 45N 140 45 E
7 Apeldoorn, Neth. ......52 13N 5 57 E
10 Apennines, Mts., Italy..44 20N 10 20 E
40 Apia, W. Samoa.......13 50S 171 50W
35 Appalachian Mts.,
U.S.A. 38 0N 80 0W
18 Aqabah, G. of Red Sea .29 31N 35 0 E
18 Ar Riyad, Si. Arabia ...24 44N 46 43 E
16 Arabian Sea, Asia .....21 0N 63 0 E
37 Aracaju, Brazil 11 0S 37 0W
11 Arad, Rumania........46 10N 21 20 E
8 Aragon, Prov., Spain...41 25N 1 0W
14 Aral Sea, Asia.........44 30N 60 0 E
14 Aralsk, U.S.S.R........46 50N 61 20 E
6 Aran, Is., Ireland 55 0N 8 30W
3 Ararat, Mount, Turkey.39 40N 44 24 E
5 Arbroath, Scotland 56 34N 2 35W
1 Arctic Ocean 78 0N 160 0W
7 Ardennes, Belgium ....50 5N 5 15 E
37 Arequipa, Peru 16 20S 71 30W
37 Argentina, Rep., S.
Amer. 35 0S 60 0W
5 Argyll, co., Scotland ...56 18N 5 15W
13 Århus, Denmark ......56 7N 10 11 E
36 Arima, Trinidad ... 10 38N 61 17W
34 Arizona, st. U.S.A. 34 20N 111 30W
35 Arkansas, st., U.S.A....35 0N 92 0W
35 Arkansas, R., U.S.A. ...38 0N 98 0W
14 Arkhangelsk, U.S.S.R. .64 40N 41 0 E
6 Arklow, Ireland 52 48N 6 10W
7 Arles, France ....43 41N 4 40 E
6 Armagh, N. Ireland....54 22N 6 40W
6 Armagh, co., N. Ire. ...54 16N 6 35W
14 Armavir, U.S.S.R. .....45 2N 41 7 E
14 Armenia, S.S.R.,
U.S.S.R. ....40 0N 41 0 E
7 Arnhem, Neth. ....51 58N 5 55 E
5 Arran, I., Scotland 55 34N 5 12W
7 Artois, Prov., France ..50 20N 2 30 E
23 Aru, Is., Indon. .... 6 0S 134 30 E
36 Aruba, I., Neth., W.I...12 30N 70 0W
13 Arvika, Swed. ....59 42N 68 30 E
18 As Salala, Muscat &
Oman ....16 59N 35 47 E
21 Asahigawa, Japan......43 45N 142 30 E
25 Ascension, I., Atlantic
Ocean 8 0S 14 15W
9 Aschaffenburg, Ger. ...49 58N 9 8 E
10 Ascoli Piceno, Italy ....42 51N 13 34 E
40 Ashburton, N.Z.......43 53S 171 48 E
17 Ashdod, Israel ....31 46N 34 39 E
21 Ashikaga, Japan ....36 28N 139 29 E
14 Ashkhabad, U.S.S.R....38 0N 57 50 E
17 Ashquelon, Israel......31 40N 34 35 E
1 Asia, Continent ....80 0N to 10 0S
30 0 E to 180 0 E
18 Asmera, Ethiopia......15 19N 38 55 E
19 Assam, st., India ......25 45N 92 30 E
14 Astrakhan U.S.S.R. ...46 25N 48 5 E
8 Asturias, Prov., Spain 43 15N 6 0W
37 Asuncion, Paraguay....25 11S 57 30W
27 Aswān, Egypt.........24 4N 32 57 E
27 Asyūt, Egypt ....27 11N 31 4 E
27 Atbara, Sudan ....17 50N 34 3 E
11 Athens, Greece ....37 58N 23 46 E
6 Athlone, Ireland 53 26N 7 57W
35 Atlanta, U.S.A. 33 50N 84 15W
40 Auckland, N.Z. ....36 52S 174 46 E
41 Auckland Is., Ant......51 0S 166 0 E
7 Aunis, Prov., France ..46 0N 0 50W
34 Austin, U.S.A. 30 20N 97 45W
38 Australia, Common- 10 35S to 43 38S
wealth of 114 0 E to 153 40 E
39 Australian Alps, Vic.,
Austral.............36 30S 148 8 E
41 Australian Dependency,
Ant................73 0S 90 0 E
9 Austria, Rep., Europe..47 30N 13 30 E
7 Auvergne, Prov., France45 15N 3 10 E
7 Avignon, France ......43 57N 4 50 E
8 Avila, Spain 40 39N 4 43W
39 Avon Downs, Austral. .21 50S 147 16 E
4 Aylesbury, Eng........51 48N 0 49W
5 Ayr & co., Scotland ...55 28N 4 37W
22 Ayutthaya, Thailand ...14 25N 100 30 E
27 Az Zaqāziq, Egypt.....30 40N 31 12 E
1 Azores, I., Atlantic Oc. 38 44N 29 0W
14 Azov, Sea of ,U.S.S.R...46 0N 36 30 E
14 Azerbaijan, S.S.R.,
U.S.S.R.............40 20N 48 0 E

B

11 Bačau, Rumania ....46 35N 26 55 E
23 Bacolod, Phil ....10 50N 123 0 E
8 Badajoz, Spain 38 50N 6 59W
8 Badalona, Spain ....41 26N 2 15 E
9 Baden-Wurttemberg,
Land, Germany .....48 33N 9 0 E
33 Baffin, I., Canada 68 0N 77 0W
21 Bafu, Japan ....34 3N 131 20 E
37 Bagé, Brazil 31 22N 54 6W
18 Baghdad, Iraq ....33 20N 44 30 E
36 Bahama Is., W. Indies..24 40N 74 0W
37 Bahia Blanca, Arg......38 35S 62 13W
27 Bahr el Ghazal, Prov.,
Sudan............. 7 0N 28 0 E
18 Bahrain, st., Asia ......26 0N 50 35 E
15 Baikal, L., U.S.S.R. ....53 0N 108 0 E
6 Baile Atha Cliath, see Dublin
8 Baixo-Alentejo, Prov.,
Portugal 38 0N 8 0W
14 Baku, U.S.S.R. ....40 25N 49 45 E
19 Balasore, India ....21 35N 87 3 E
9 Balaton, L., Hungary...46 50N 17 40 E
8 Balearic Is., Spain .....39 30N 3 0 E
23 Bali, I., Indonesia...... 8 20S 115 0 E
23 Balikpapan, Indonesia .. 1 10S 116 55 E
14 Balkhash, L., U.S.S.R. ..46 0S 74 50 E
39 Ballarat, Australia .....37 33S 143 50 E
6 Ballina, Ireland........54 7N 9 10W
6 Ballinasloe, Ireland 53 20N 8 12W
6 Ballymena, N. Ireland ..54 53N 6 18W
13 Baltic Sea, Europe .....56 0N 20 0 E
35 Baltimore, U.S.A. 39 18N 76 37W
26 Bamako, Mali 12 48N 7 59W
4 Banbury, England 52 4N 1 21W
22 Banda Atjeh, Indon. .... 5 35N 95 20 E
18 Banda Abbas, Iran .....27 15N 56 15 E
23 Bandjarmasin, Indon. .. 3 20S 114 25 E
22 Bandung, Indonesia.... 6 36S 107 48 E
5 Banff, Scotland........57 40N 2 32W
5 Banff, co., Scotland 57 23N 3 10W
19 Bangalore, India.......12 59N 77 40 E
28 Bangassou, Cen. Afr.
Rep................ 4 55N 23 55 E
22 Bangka, I., Indonesia... 2 0S 105 50 E
22 Bangkok, Thailand.....13 45N 100 35 E
6 Bangor, N. Ireland 54 40N 5 40W
4 Bangor, Wales 53 13N 4 9W
28 Bangui, Cen. Afr. Rep.. 4 23N 18 35 E
27 Bani Suwayf, Egypt ....29 9N 31 5 E
41 Banks I., Canada 73 30N 120 0W
36 Barbados, I., W.I. 13 0N 59 30W
8 Barcelona, Spain ......41 21N 2 10 E
37 Barcelona, Venezuela ..10 10N 64 40W
27 Bardai, Chad ....21 25N 17 0 E
25 Bardera, Somali Rep. .. 2 20N 42 27 E
19 Bareilly, India ....28 22N 79 27 E
14 Barents Sea, Arctic Oc. 73 0N 39 0 E
10 Bari, Italy ....41 6N 16 52 E
10 Barletta, Italy.........41 20N 16 17 E
14 Barnaul, U.S.S.R.......53 20N 83 40 E
4 Barnsley, England 53 33N 1 29W
4 Barnstaple, England ...51 5N 4 3W
19 Baroda, India ....22 20N 73 10 E
37 Barquisimeto, Ven..... 9 58N 69 13W
5 Barra Is., Scotland 57 0N 7 30W
37 Barranquilla, Colombia 11 0N 74 50W
4 Barrow in Furness, Eng. 54 8N 3 15W
37 Bartica, Guyana 6 25N 58 40W
10 Basilicata, Reg., Italy...40 30N 16 0 E
4 Basingstoke, England ..51 15N 1 5W
23 Basitan, I., Phil. .... 6 20N 122 30 E
9 Basle, Switzerland .....47 33N 7 34 E
8 Basque Provinces, Spain41 55N 2 40W
36 Basse Terre,
Guadeloupe 16 0N 61 40W
19 Bassein, Burma ....16 0N 94 30 E
7 Bastia, Corsica, Fr. ....42 40N 9 30 E
28 Bata, Rio Muni........ 1 57N 9 50 E
4 Bath, England.........51 22N 2 22W
26 Bathurst, Gambia 13 28N 16 40W
35 Baton Rouge, U.S.A....30 30N 91 5W
22 Batu, Is., Indonesia .... 0 30S 98 25 E
22 Batu Pahat, Malaya .... 1 50N 102 56 E
14 Batumi, U.S.S.R. ......41 30N 41 30 E
26 Bauchi, Nigeria ....10 22N 9 48 E
9 Bavaria, Land, Germany49 8N 11 30 E
20 Bayinhot, China........39 55N 105 35 E
7 Bayonne, France 43 30N 1 28W
37 Beagle Chan., Chile/
Arg................54 50S 69 0W
7 Bearn, Prov., France...43 9N 0 50W
41 Beaufort Sea, Alaska...70 30N 146 0W
35 Beaumont, U.S.A. 30 5N 94 8W
4 Bedford, England......52 8N 0 29W
4 Bedford, co., England ..52 4N 0 28W
17 Beer Sheva, Israel .....31 14N 34 47 E
29 Beira, Mozam. ....19 50S 34 52 E
8 Beira Alta, Prov., Port. 40 35N 7 35W
8 Beira-Baixa, Prov.,
Portugal 39 50N 7 35W
8 Beira Litoral, Prov.,
Portugal 40 5N 8 30W
2 Beirut, Lebanon.......33 53N 35 31 E
37 Belém, Brazil 1 20S 48 30W
6 Belfast, N. Ireland 54 35N 5 36W
7 Belfort, France........47 38N 6 50 E
7 Belgium, King., Europe 51 30N 5 0 E
31 Belize, Br. Honduras ..17 25N 88 0W
11 Belgrade, Y.-Slav. .....44 50N 20 37 E
22 Belitung, I., Indonesia.. 3 10S 107 50 E
7 Belle I., France........47 20N 3 10W
19 Bellary, India ....15 10N 76 56 E
37 Belo Horizonte, Brazil .20 0S 44 0W
5 Ben Nevis, Mt., Scot. ..56 48N 5 0W
19 Benares, see Varanasi, India
19 Bengal, Bay of ,India ...17 0N 89 0 E
27 Benghazi, Libya ....32 10N 20 3 E
29 Benguela, Angola......12 37S 13 25 E
26 Benin City, Nigeria.... 6 20N 5 31 E
29 Benoni, S. Africa ......26 11S 28 18 E
18 Berbera, Somali Rep. ..10 30N 45 2 E
37 Berbice, R., Guyana ... 5 20N 58 10W
18 Bereda, Somali Rep. ...11 52N 51 5 E
14 Berezniki, U.S.S.R. ....59 25N 56 5 E
10 Bergamo, Italy ....45 42N 9 40 E
13 Bergen, Norway ......60 23N 5 27 E
19 Berhampur, India .....19 15N 84 54 E
1 Bering Sea, U.S.S.R. ...58 0N 167 0 E
31 Bering Str., U.S.S.R./
U.S.A. 66 0N 170 0W
34 Berkeley, U.S.A. 38 0N 122 20W
4 Berkshire, co., Eng. ...51 30N 1 20W
9 Berlin, Germany ......52 32N 13 24 E
30 Bermuda, I., Atlantic
Ocean 32 45N 65 0W
9 Bern, Switzerland .....46 57N 7 28 E
5 Berwick, co., Scotland .55 46N 2 30W
4 Berwick-upon-Tweed,
England 55 47N 2 0W
7 Besancon, France......47 15N 6 0 E
17 Bet Shean, Israel ......32 30N 35 30 E
17 Bethlehem, Jordan ....31 43N 35 12 E
4 Bexhill, England.......50 50N 0 29 E
7 Béziers, France ....43 20N 3 12 E
19 Bhaunagar, India ......21 45N 72 10 E
19 Bhutan, st., Asia ......27 25N 89 50 E
13 Bialystok, Poland......53 10N 23 10 E
7 Biarritz, France 43 29N 1 33W
9 Biel, Switzerland ......47 8N 7 14 E
9 Bielefeld, Germany ....52 2N 8 31 E
22 Bien Hoa, S. Vietnam ..11 3N 106 53 E
19 Bihar, tn. & st.. India ..25 5N 85 40 E
19 Bikaner, India.........28 2N 73 18 E
8 Bilboa, Spain 43 16N 2 56W
27 Bilma, Niger..........18 50N 13 30 E
17 Bira, Jordan ....31 55N 35 12 E
4 Birkenhead, England...53 24N 3 1W
4 Birmingham, England ..52 30N 1 55W
35 Birmingham, U.S.A. ...33 40N 86 50W
2 Biscay, Bay of, Atlantic
Ocean 45 0N 2 0W
4 Bishop Auckland, Eng. .54 40N 1 40W
1 Bismark Arch., Terr.
of New Guinea ..... 3 30S 148 30 E
11 Bitolj, Y.-Slav. ....41 5N 21 21 E
27 Bizerte, Tunisia ....37 15N 9 50 E
9 Black Forest, Germany.48 0N 8 0 E
2 Black Sea, Europe .....43 30N 35 0 E
26 Black Volta, R., Ghana . 9 0N 2 40W
4 Blackburn, England....53 44N 2 30 E
4 Blackpool, England 53 48N 3 3W
6 Blackwater, R., Ireland.53 46N 7 0W
6 Blackwater, R., N. Ire. .54 25N 7 0W
36 Blanquilla, I., Ven......12 0N 64 40W
29 Blantyre, Malawi ......15 45S 35 0 E
40 Blenheim, N.Z. ....41 38S 174 5 E
29 Bloemfontein, S. Africa 29 6S 26 14 E
34 Blue Mts., U.S.A.......45 30N 118 10W
36 Bluefields, Nicaragua ..12 0N 83 50W
37 Blumenau, Brazil 27 0S 49 0W
4 Blyth, England 55 8N 1 32W
26 Bobo-Dioulasso, Upper
Volta 11 8N 4 13W
9 Bochum, Germany ....51 28N 7 12 E
12 Boden, Sweden ....65 50N 21 42 E
6 Boggeragh, Mts., Ire ..52 2N 8 55W
4 Bognor Regis, England .50 47N 0 40W
37 Bogota, Colombia 4 34N 74 0W
9 Bohemian Forest, Cz ..49 20N 13 0 E
23 Bohol, I., Phil .... 9 58N 124 20 E
37 Bolivia, Rep., S. Amer..17 6S 64 0W
13 Böllnäs, Sweden.......61 22N 16 28 E
10 Bologna, Italy ....44 30N 11 20 E
4 Bolton, England 53 35N 2 26W
10 Bolzano, Italy ....46 30N 11 20 E
19 Bombay, India ....18 55N 72 50 E
36 Bonaire,I., Neth. W.I. .12 10N 68 15W
33 Bonavista, Canada 48 40N 53 5W
1 Bonin Is., Pacific Oc....27 0N 142 0 E
9 Bonn, Germany ....50 43N 7 6 E
33 Boothia, G. of, Canada .70 0N 90 0W
4 Bootle, England 53 28N 3 1W
13 Borås, Sweden ....57 42N 13 1 E
7 Bordeaux, France 44 50N 0 36W
13 Borlange, Sweden .....60 28N 15 25 E
22 Borneo, I., E. Indies ... 1 0N 115 0 E
13 Bornholm, I., Denmark 55 8N 14 55 E
10 Bosnia & Hercegovina,
Prov., Y.-Slav. ......44 40N 17 0 E
35 Boston, U.S.A.........42 20N 71 0W
13 Bothnia, Gulf of, Eur...63 0N 21 0 E
11 Botoşani, Rumania ....47 42N 26 41 E
29 Botswana, st., Africa...23 0S 24 0 E
26 Bouake, Ivory Coast ... 7 40N 4 55W
7 Boulogne, France......50 42N 1 36 E
7 Bourbonnais, Prov., Fr. 46 28N 3 0 E
7 Bourges, France.......47 5N 2 22 E
7 Bourgogne, Reg., Fr. ..47 0N 4 30 E
4 Bournemouth, England 50 43N 1 53W
6 Boyne, R., Ireland 53 43N 6 15W
10 Brač, I., Y.-Slav........43 20N 16 40 E
4 Bradford, England 53 47N 1 45W
8 Braga, Portugal 41 35N 8 32W
11 Braila, Rumania ....45 19N 27 59 E
9 Brandenburg, E. Ger...52 24N 12 33 E
37 Brasilia, Fed. Dist.,
Brazil..............15 30S 47 30W
11 Braşov, Rumania ......45 39N 25 35 E
9 Bratislava, Cz. ....48 10N 17 7 E
25 Brava, Somali Rep. .... 1 20N 44 8 E
6 Bray, Ireland 53 12N 6 6W
37 Brazil, Rep , S. Amer. 5 0N to 34 0S
35 0W to 74 0W
28 Brazzaville, Congo (Fr.) 4 9S 15 12 E
5 Brechin, Scotland 56 44N 2 40W
4 Brecknock, co., Wales .51 58N 3 25W
7 Breda, Neth. ....51 35N 4 45 E
9 Bremen, Germany.....53 4N 8 47 E
9 Bremerhaven, Ger.....53 34N 8 35 E
9 Brenner Pass, Alps ....47 0N 11 30 E
10 Brescia, Italy..........45 33N 10 13 E
7 Brest, France 48 24N 4 31W
7 Bretagne, Prov., Fr. ...48 0N 3 0W
35 Bridgeport, U.S.A. 41 12N 73 12W
36 Bridgetown, Barbados .13 0N 59 30W
4 Brighton, England 44 3N 77 44W
11 Brindisi, Italy ....40 39N 17 55 E
39 Brisbane, Australia ....27 25S 152 54 E
4 Bristol, England 51 26N 2 35W
4 Bristol Chan., U.K.....51 18N 3 30W
1 Br. Antarctic Terr.,
Antarctica..........67 0S 40 0W
32 British Columbia,
Prov., Canada.......55 0N 125 15W
31 Br. Honduras, Col.,
Central America 17 0N 88 30W
9 Brno, Cz. ....49 10N 16 35 E
39 Broken Hill, Austral. ..31 58S 141 29 E
7 Brugge, Belgium ......51 13N 3 13 E
23 Brunei, st. & tn.,
East Indies .... 4 52N 115 0 E
9 Brunswick, Germany ..52 15N 10 30W
7 Brussels, Belgium .....50 51N 4 21 E
14 Bryansk, U.S.S.R. .....53 15N 34 20 E
37 Bucaramanga, Colombia 7 0N 73 0W
11 Bucharest, Rumania ...44 27N 26 10 E
4 Buckingham, co., Eng. .52 0N 0 59W
2 Budapest, Hungary ....47 29N 19 5 E
37 Buenos Aires, Arg. 34 30S 58 20W
35 Buffalo, U.S.A.........42 55N 78 50W
29 Bukama, Congo .... 9 10S 25 50 E
14 Bukhara, U.S.S.R. .....39 50N 64 10 E
28 Bukoba, Tanz. .... 1 20S 31 49 E
29 Bulawayo, Rhodesia ...20 7S 28 32 E
11 Bulgaria, Rep., Europe .42 35N 34 30 E
22 Bunguran, Is., Indon. .. 4 0N 108 0 E
11 Burgas, Bulgaria.......42 33N 27 29 E
9 Burgenland, Prov.,
Austria ....47 20N 16 20 E
8 Burgos, Spain.........42 21N 3 42W
19 Burma, Rep., Asia .....21 0N 96 30 E
2 Bursa, Turkey ....40 15N 29 5 E
4 Burton-on-Trent, Eng. .52 48N 1 39W
23 Buru, I., Indon. .... 3 30S 126 30 E
28 Burundi, st., Africa .... 3 0S 30 0 E
4 Bury St. Edmunds, Eng.52 15N 0 42 E
18 Bushehr (Bushire),
Iran ....28 55N 50 55 E
28 Buta, Congo .... 2 50N 24 53 E
28 Butare, Rwanda....... 2 31S 29 52 E
9 Bydgoszcz, Poland.....53 10N 18 0 E
41 Byrd Land, Ant........80 0S 125 0W
9 Bytom, Poland ....50 25N 19 0 E

C

28 Cabinda, Angola ...... 5 40S 12 11 E
8 Caceres, Spain 39 26N 6 23W
37 Cachoeira, Brazil......12 30S 39 0W
8 Cadiz, Spain 36 30N 6 20W
8 Cadiz, Gulf of, Spain...36 35N 6 20W
7 Caen, France 49 10N 0 22W
4 Caernavon, Wales.....53 8N 4 17W
4 Caernarvon Bay, Wales 53 4N 4 40W
4 Caernarvon, co., Wales 53 5N 4 10W
4 Caerphilly, Wales 51 34N 3 13W
10 Cagliari, Sardinia, Italy .39 15N 9 6 E
36 Caicos Is., W. Indies...21 40N 71 40W
27 Cairo, Egypt..........30 2N 31 12 E
5 Caithness, co., Scot. ...58 25N 3 25W
26 Calabar, Nigeria ...... 4 57N 8 20 E
10 Calabria, Reg., Italy ...39 4N 16 30 E
7 Calais, France.........50 57N 1 56 E
37 Calamar, Colombia 10 15N 74 55W
23 Calbayog, Phil... 12 7N 124 37 E
19 Calcutta, India ....22 36N 88 24 E
32 Calgary, Canada.......51 0N 114 10W
37 Cali, Colombia........ 3 25N 76 35W
34 California, st., U.S.A. ..37 0N 120 0W
37 Callao, Peru 12 0S 77 0W
10 Caltanissetta, Sicily, It..37 30N 14 3 E
29 Calvinia, S. Africa .....31 28S 19 45 E
36 Camagüey, Cuba 21 20N 78 0W
22 Cambodia, st., Asia ....12 15N 105 0 E
4 Camborne, England ...50 13N 5 18W
4 Cambridge, England ...52 13N 0 8 E
4 Cambridgeshire & Isle
of Ely, co., England ..52 15N 0 5 E

Map
28 Cameroon, Rep.
West Africa .... 5 0N 12 30 E
10 Campania, Reg., It. ....40 50N 14 45 E
37 Campinas. Brazil 22 50S 47 0W
37 Campos, Brazil.........21 50S 41 20W
32 Canada, st., N. Amer. .60 0N 100 0W
36 Canal Zone, Panama... 9 0N 79 45W
26 Canary Is., Atlantic Oc.29 30N 17 0W
39 Canberra, Australia ...35 15S 149 8 E
7 Cannes, France ....43 32N 7 0 E
8 Cantabrian Mts., Sp....43 0N 5 10W
4 Canterbury, England ..51 17N 1 5 E
40 Canterbury Bight, N.Z.44 16S 171 55 E
20 Canton, China ....23 15N 113 15 E
35 Canton, U.S.A. 40 47N 81 22W
36 Cap Haitien, Haiti.....19 40N 72 20W
29 Cape Province, Prov.,
South Africa........32 0S 23 0 E
29 Cape Town, S. Afr.....33 56S 18 28 E
1 Cape Verde Is.,
Atlantic Ocean.......17 10N 25 20W
39 Cape York Pen.,
Austral.............13 30S 142 30 E
17 Capernaum, (site),
Israel ....32 54N 35 32 E
10 Capri, I., Italy.........40 34N 14 15 E
37 Caracas, Ven..........10 30N 66 50W
4 Cardiff, Wales 51 28N 3 11W
4 Cardigan, co., Wales...52 18N 4 0W
4 Cardigan Bay, Wales ..52 30N 4 30W
36 Caribbean Sea,
West Indies 15 0N 75 0W
9 Carinthia, Prov., Aust..46 52N 13 30 E
4 Carlisle, England 54 54N 2 55W
6 Carlow & co., Ireland..52 50N 6 58W
4 Carmarthen, co., Wales53 40N 4 18W
17 Carmel, Mount, Israel..32 45N 35 3 E
1 Caroline Is., Pacific Oc. 8 0N 150 0 E
2 Carpathians, Mts., Eur..49 0N 23 0 E
39 Carpentaria,
Gulf of, Australia....14 0S 139 0 E
10 Carrara, Italy ....44 5N 10 7 E
34 Carson City, U.S.A. ...39 0N 119 40W
37 Cartagena, Colombia ..10 20N 75 30W
8 Cartagena, Spain 37 38N 0 59W
36 Cartago, Costa Rica ... 9 50N 84 0W
37 Carúpano, Ven........10 45N 63 15W
26 Casablanca, Morocco ..33 30N 7 37W
14 Caspian Sea, U.S.S.R. ..43 0N 50 0 E
8 Castellón, Spain.......39 58N 0 3W
6 Castlebar, Ireland 53 52N 9 20W
36 Castries, St. Lucia,
West Indies 14 0N 60 50W
8 Catalonia, Prov., Spain .41 40N 1 15 E
37 Catamarca, Arg. 28 30S 65 50W
10 Catánia, Sicily, Italy ...37 31N 15 4 E
10 Catanzaro ....38 53N 16 36 E
15 Caucasus, Ra, U.S.S.R. .43 0N 44 0 E
6 Cavan & co., Ireland...54 0N 7 22W
37 Cayenne, Fr. Guiana... 5 0N 52 18W
36 Cayman Is., W. Indies .19 40N 79 50W
23 Cebu, tn. & I., Phil. ...10 30N 124 0 E
23 Celebes Sea, Asia ..... 3 0N 123 0 E
9 Celle, Germany ....52 37N 10 4 E
28 Central Africa, st., Afr. 7 0N 20 0 E
15 Central Siberian
Plateau, U.S.S.R. .....65 0N 105 0 E
23 Ceram, I., Indonesia ... 3 10S 129 0 E
10 Cerignola, Italy ....41 17N 15 53 E
9 České Budějovice, Cz. .48 55N 14 25 E
26 Ceuta, Morocco 25 52N 5 26W
19 Ceylon, st., Asia ...... 7 30N 80 50 E
27 Chad, st., Africa ......12 0N 17 0 E
1 Chagos Arch., Ind. Oc.. 6 0S 72 0 E
19 Chambal, R., India.....26 0N 76 55 E
20 Chamdo Area, Tibet,
China..............31 10N 97 35 E
7 Champagne, Prov., Fr. .49 0N 4 40 E
20 Changchow, China .....31 45N 120 0 E
20 Changchun, China.....43 58N 125 9 E
20 Changhua, Taiwan .....24 2N 120 30 E
20 Changsha, China ......28 5N 113 1 E
7 Channel Is., Br. Isles...49 30N 2 40W
20 Chaochow, China .....23 40N 116 30 E
14 Chardzhou, U.S.S.R....39 0N 63 20 E
35 Charleston, U.S.A. 32 55N 80 0W
35 Charlotte, U.S.A. 35 16N 80 46W
9 Charlottenburg,
East Germany ......52 30N 13 21 E
33 Charlottetown, Can. ..46 19N 63 3W
7 Chartres, France ......48 29N 1 30 E
33 Chatham, Canada 47 2N 65 28W
4 Chatham, England .....51 22N 0 32 E
35 Chattanooga, U.S.A....35 0N 85 20W
20 Chefoo, China ....37 30N 121 25 E
21 Cheju Do., S. Korea ...33 30N 126 30 E
20 Chekiang, Prov., China 29 20N 120 0 E
4 Chelmsford, England ..51 44N 0 29 E
4 Cheltenham, England ..51 53N 2 7W
14 Chelyabinsk, U.S.S.R...55 10N 61 35 E
20 Chengchow, China ....34 45N 113 45 E
20 Chengtu, China ....30 40N 104 12 E
7 Cherbourg, France 49 39N 1 40W
14 Chernovtsy, U.S.S.R. ..48 0N 26 0 E
4 Cheshire, co., England .53 14N 2 30W
4 Chester, England......53 12N 2 53W
4 Chesterfield, England ..53 14N 1 26W
22 Chiang Mai, Thailand ..18 55N 98 55 E
20 Chiayi, Taiwan ....23 29N 120 25 E
21 Chiba, Japan..........35 30N 140 7 E
35 Chicago, U.S.A........41 56N 87 50W
4 Chichester, England ...50 50N 0 47W
37 Chiclayo, Peru 6 42S 79 50W
33 Chicoutimi, Canada ...48 28N 71 5W
37 Chile, Rep., S. Amer. 17 30S to 55 0S
71 15W
37 Chiloé, I., Chile 42 50S 73 45W
4 Chiltern Hills, Eng.....51 44N 0 42W
14 Chimkent, U.S.S.R.....42 40N 69 25 E
20 China, Rep., Asia ...55 0N to 18 30 N
70 0S to 133 0 E
20 Chinchow, China.......41 10N 121 10 E
29 Chinde, Mozambique ..18 45S 36 30 E
19 Chindwin, R., Burma ..22 30N 95 0 E
26 Chinguetti, Mauritania .20 25N 12 15W
20 Chinkiang, China......32 15N 119 30 E
19 Chins Division, Burma .22 0N 93 0 E
20 Chinwangtao, China ...40 0N 119 35 E
37 Chiquinquira, Colombia 5 50N 74 0W
15 Chita, U.S.S.R.........52 0N 113 25 E
36 Chitré, Panama 7 59N 80 27W
19 Chittagong, E. Pakistan 22 19N 91 55 E
36 Choluteca, Honduras ..13 20N 87 14W
21 Chongjin, N. Korea ...41 40N 129 40 E
37 Chonos Arch., Chile...45 0S 75 0W
9 Chorzów, Poland......50 18N 19 0 E
40 Christchurch, N.Z......43 33S 172 39 E
1 Christmas I., Indian Oc.10 0S 105 40 E

Map
21 Chuchon, S. Korea ....37 55N 127 30 E
20 Chuchow, China ....35 30N 118 40 E
20 Chungking, China .....29 35N 106 50 E
35 Cincinnati, U.S.A......39 8N 84 25W
37 Ciudad Bolivar, Ven. .. 8 5N 63 30W
30 Ciudad Juárez, Mexico .31 40N 106 28W
5 Clackmannan, co., Scot.56 10N 3 47W
4 Clacton-on-Sea, Eng....51 47N 1 10 E
6 Clare, co., Ireland 52 52N 8 55W
4 Cleethorpes, England .53 33N 0 20W
7 Clermont Ferrand, Fr. .45 46N 3 4 E
35 Cleveland, U.S.A. 41 28N 81 43W
6 Clonmel, Ireland 52 22N 7 42W
11 Cluj, Rumania ....46 47N 23 38 E
5 Clyde, Firth of, Scot. ..55 20N 5 0W
5 Clyde, R., Scotland 55 46N 3 58W
5 Clydebank, Scotland ...55 54N 4 25W
5 Coatbridge, Scotland ..55 52N 4 2W
33 Cobalt, Canada 47 25N 79 42W
31 Coban, Guatemala......15 30N 90 21W
6 Cobh, Ireland.........51 50N 8 18W
19 Cocanada, India ....16 55N 82 20 E
37 Cochabamba, Bolivia ..17 15S 66 20W
33 Cochrane, Canada 49 0N 81 0W
1 Cocos Is., Indian Oc....12 12S 96 54 E
19 Coimbatore, India......11 2N 76 59 E
8 Coimbra, Portugal 40 15N 8 27W
4 Colchester, England ...51 54N 0 55 E
6 Coleraine, N. Ireland ..55 8N 6 40 E
5 Coll, I., Scotland 56 40N 6 3W
9 Cologne, Germany ....50 56N 6 57 E
37 Colombia, Rep.,
South America...... 3 45N 73 0W
19 Colombo, Ceylon ..... 6 56N 79 58 E
36 Colón, Panama........ 9 20N 80 0W
34 Colorado, R., U.S.A....33 30N 114 30W
34 Colorado, st., U.S.A. ..39 5N 104 45W
35 Colorado Springs,
U.S.A..............38 50N 104 50W
35 Columbia, U.S.A.......34 0N 81 0W
34 Columbia, R., U.S.A. ..51 50N 118 0W
35 Columbus, Georgia,
U.S.A..............32 30N 84 58W
35 Columbus, Ohio,
U.S.A..............39 57N 83 1W
4 Colwyn Bay, Wales 53 17N 3 44W
10 Como, Italy ....45 48N 9 5 E
25 Comoro Is., Indian Oc..12 0S 44 0 E
26 Conakry, Guinea 9 29N 13 49W
37 Concepción, Chile......36 50S 73 0W
37 Concepcion, Paraguay .23 30S 57 20W
37 Concordia, Arg........31 20S 58 2W
28 Congo, st., Africa ..... 3 0S 22 0 E
28 Congo, st., (Fr.) Africa . 2 0S 16 0 E
28 Congo, R., Congo ...... 2 0N 23 0 E
6 Connaught, Prov., Ire. .53 45N 9 0W
35 Connecticut, st., U.S.A.41 40N 72 40W
6 Connemara, Reg., Ire. .44 14N 28 38 E
11 Constanta, Rumania ...44 14N 28 38 E
26 Constantine, Algeria...36 25N 6 30 E
40 Cook Is., Pacific Oc....22 0S 157 0W
13 Copenhagen, Denmark.55 41N 12 34 E
32 Coppermine, Canada ..68 0N 116 0W
39 Coral Sea, Pac. Oc.....15 0S 150 0 E
37 Cordóba, Argentina ...31 20S 64 10W
8 Cordóba, Spain 37 50N 4 50W
31 Cordova, Alaska 33 45N 87 12W
11 Corinth, Gulf of, Gr. ..38 10N 22 40 E
36 Corinto, Nicaragua 12 30N 87 10W
6 Cork & co., Ireland....51 54N 8 30W
36 Corn Is., Cent. Amer. .12 0S 83 0W
4 Cornwall, co., Eng......50 26N 4 40W
34 Corpus Christi, U.S.A..27 50N 97 28W
37 Corrientes, Arg. 27 30S 58 45W
7 Corsica, I., Medit. S.,
Dépt., France.......42 0N 9 0 E
36 Costa Rica, st.,
South America.......10 0N 84 0W
26 Cotonou, Dahomey ... 6 20N 2 25 E
4 Cotswold Hills, Eng....51 42N 2 10W
9 Cottbus, E. Germany ..51 44N 14 20 E
4 Coventry, England 52 25N 1 31W
4 Cowes, England.......50 45N 1 18W
31 Cozumel, I., Mexico ...20 30N 86 40W
11 Craiova, Rumania .....44 21N 23 48 E
10 Cremona, Italy.......45 8N 10 2 E
10 Cres, I., Yugoslavia ....44 50N 14 25 E
10 Crete, I., Greece.......35 15N 25 0 E
4 Crewe, England 53 6N 2 28W
14 Crimea, Pen., U.S.S.R. .45 0N 34 0 E
11 Crna Gora (Montenegro)
Prov., Yugoslavia....43 0N 19 30 E
10 Croatia, Prov., Y.-Slav .45 40N 17 0 E
5 Cromarty, Scotland ...57 40N 4 2W
36 Cuba, I., Rep.,
W. Indies 22 0N 79 0W
37 Cucuta, Colombia 8 0N 72 30W
37 Cuenca, Ecuador 2 50S 79 9W
8 Cuenca, Spain 45 0N 2 10W
37 Cuiaba, Brazil.........15 30S 56 0W
37 Cumana, Venezuela....10 30N 64 5W
4 Cumberland, co., Eng. .54 44N 2 54W
36 Curaçao, I., Neth.
West Indies 12 10N 69 0W
37 Curitiba Brazil 25 20S 49 10W
37 Cusco, Peru 13 32S 72 0W
19 Cuttack, India ....20 25N 85 57 E
2 Cyprus, I., Medit. Sea ..35 0N 33 0 E
2 Czechoslovakia, st.,
Europe ....49 0N 17 0 E

D

22 Da-Nang, S. Vietnam ..16 10N 108 7 E
18 Dabra Tabor,
Ethiopia............11 50N 37 58 E
19 Dacca, E. Pakistan ....23 43N 90 26 E
18 Dahlak Kebir, I.,
Red Sea.............15 50N 40 10 E
26 Dahomey, st., W. Afr.. 8 0N 2 0 E
26 Dakar, Senegal 14 34N 17 29W
35 Dallas, U.S.A..........32 50N 96 50W
27 Damanhûr, Egypt .....31 0N 30 30 E
2 Damascus see Esh Sham
27 Damietta, Egypt ......36 10N 54 17 E
38 Dampier, Arch.,
Australia ....20 38S 116 32 E
2 Danube, R., Europe ...45 0N 28 20 E
19 Darbhanga, India......26 15N 86 3 E
28 Dar-es-Salaam, Tanz.... 6 50S 39 12 E
19 Darjeeling, India ......27 3N 88 18 E
39 Darling, R., Austral....31 0S 144 30 E
4 Darlington, England ...54 33N 1 33W
9 Darmstadt, Germany ..49 51N 8 40 E
27 Darnah, Libya ....32 45N 22 39 E
33 Dartmouth, Canada ...44 40N 63 30W
4 Dartmouth, England ...50 21N 3 35W
38 Darwin, Australia .....12 20S 130 50 E
32 Dauphin, Canada 51 15N 100 5W

Map
7 Dauphine, Prov., Fr....45 15N 5 25 E
23 Davao, Philippines..... 7 0N 125 40 E
36 David, Panama 8 30N 82 30W
10 Davos, Switzerland ....46 48N 9 49 E
32 Dawson, Canada 64 10N 139 30W
35 Dayton, U.S.A. 39 45N 84 10W
29 De Aar, S. Africa.......30 39S 24 0 E
27 De Béhagle, Chad ..... 9 25N 16 30 E
17 Dead Sea, Jordan/Isr. ..31 30N 35 30 E
4 Deal, England.........51 13N 1 25 E
2 Debrecen, Hungary ...47 33N 21 42 E
35 Delaware, st., U.S.A. ..39 0N 75 40W
19 Delhi, India...........28 38N 77 17 E
4 Denbigh, co., Wales ...53 8N 3 30W
13 Denmark, King, Eur. ...55 30N 9 0 E
34 Denver, U.S.A. 39 48N 105 0W
4 Derby & co., England ..52 55N 1 28W
35 Des Moines, U.S.A.....41 29N 93 40W
26 Dessa, Niger ....14 34N 1 3 E
9 Dessau, E. Germany ...51 49N 12 15 E
35 Detroit, U.S.A. 42 20N 83 5W
4 Devon, co., England ...50 45N 3 45W
40 Devonport, N.Z........36 49S 174 49 E
18 Dezful, Iran ....32 22N 48 30 E
18 Dhamar, Yemen ......14 29N 44 27 E
29 Diego Suarez, Malagasy
Republic ....12 25S 49 20 E
7 Diekirch, Luxemburg ..49 52N 6 10 E
7 Dieppe, France ....49 54N 1 4 E
7 Dijon, France ....47 20N 5 0 E
10 Dinaric Alps, Y.-Slav...44 0N 17 30 E
18 Dire Dawa, Ethiopia ... 9 35N 41 45 E
35 District of Columbia,
st., U.S.A...........39 0N 77 0W
22 Djakarta, Indonesia.... 6 9S 106 49 E
18 Djibouti, Fr. Terr. of
the Afars and the
Issas, ...11 30N 43 3 E
14 Dnepr, R., U.S.S.R.....50 0N 31 0 E
14 Dnepropetrovsk,
U.S.S.R.............48 30N 35 0 E
11 Dodecanese, Is., Gr....36 50N 27 0 E
28 Dodoma, Tanz. .... 6 5S 35 42 E
36 Dominica, I.,
Windward Is........15 20N 61 20W
36 Dominican Rep.,
West Indies 19 0N 70 30W
4 Doncaster, England....53 31N 1 9W
6 Donegal & co., Ire.....54 39N 8 8W
14 Donetsk U.S.S.R.......48 7N 37 50 E
22 Dong Hoi, N. Vietnam .17 18N 106 36 E
27 Dongola, Sudan ....19 9N 30 22 E
4 Dorchester, England...50 42N 2 28W
7 Dordrecht, Neth. 51 48N 4 39 E
5 Dornoch, Scotland 57 52N 4 0W
4 Dorset, co., England...50 48N 2 25W
9 Dortmund, Germany ..51 32N 7 28 E
28 Douala, Cameroon .... 4 0N 9 45 E
4 Douglas, I. of Man 54 9N 4 29W
8 Douro-Litoral, Prov.,
Portugal 41 10N 8 20W
4 Dover, England ....51 7N 1 19 E
6 Down, co., N. Ireland .54 20N 6 0W
1 Drake Str., S. Oc.......58 0S 68 0W
13 Drammen, Norway ....59 42N 10 12 E
9 Dresden, E. Germany ..51 2N 13 45 E
6 Drogheda, Ireland 53 45N 6 20W
6 Dublin (Baile Atha
Claith) Ireland 53 20N 6 18W
6 Dublin, co., Ireland....53 25N 6 20W
11 Dubrovnik, Y.-Slav. ...42 39N 18 6 E
4 Dudley, England 52 30N 2 5W
10 Dugi Otok, I., Y.-Slav. .44 0N 15 5 E
9 Duisburg, Germany ...51 27N 6 42 E
5 Dumfries, Scotland 55 4N 3 37W
5 Dumfries, co., Scot. ...55 12N 3 30W
6 Dun Laoghaire, Ireland.53 17N 6 9W
5 Dumbarton, co., Scot...56 4N 4 42W
6 Dundalk, Ireland 53 55N 6 45W
5 Dundee, Scotland 56 29N 3 0W
40 Dunedin, N.Z..........45 50S 170 33 E
5 Dunfermline, Scotland .56 5N 3 28W
6 Dungannon, N. Ire.....54 30N 6 47W
6 Dungarvan, Ireland 52 6N 7 40W
7 Dunkerque, France ....51 2N 2 20 E
4 Dunstable, England 51 53N 0 31W
29 Durban, S. Africa .....29 49S 31 1 E
4 Durham, England 54 47N 1 34W
4 Durham, co., England ..54 42N 1 45W
11 Durrës, Albania.......41 19N 19 28 E
14 Dushanbe, U.S.S.R.....38 50N 68 50 E
9 Dusseldorf, Germany ..51 15N 6 46 E
31 Dutch Harbor,
Aleutian Is..........53 40N 166 30W
14 Dzerzhinsk, U.S.S.R....56 15N 43 15 E
20 Dzhargalantu, Mong. ..48 0N 91 20 E
20 Dzhibkhalantu, Mong. .47 50N 96 50 E

E

20 East China Sea, Asia ...27 0N 125 0 E
4 East Grinstead, Eng. ...51 8N 0 1W
22 East Indies, Asia....... 0 0N 120 0 E
29 East London, S. Afr. ...33 0S 27 55 E
5 East Lothian, co., Scot..56 0N 2 40W
15 East Siberian Sea,
U.S.S.R.............73 0N 160 0 E
4 Eastbourne, England ...50 46N 0 18 E
19 Eastern Ghats, Mts.,
India...............15 0N 80 0 E
4 Eastleigh, England 50 55N 1 21W
4 Ebbw Vale, Wales 51 47N 3 12W
37 Ecuador, Rep.,
South America.......22 0S 79 0W
5 Edinburgh, Scotland ...55 57N 3 12W
32 Edmonton, Canada 53 30N 113 30W
13 Egersund, Norway ....58 26N 5 59 E
27 Egypt (U.A.R.) st.,
N. Africa ....25 0N 30 0 E
7 Eindhoven, Neth. .....51 26N 5 30 E
26 El Aiun, Sp. Sahara 27 10N 8 0W
18 El Dere, Somali Rep. .. 3 58N 47 17 E
27 El Obeid, Sudan........13 8N 30 10 E
34 El Paso, U.S.A.........31 50N 106 30W
10 Elba, I., Italy ....42 48N 10 15 E
9 Elbe, R., Germany .....53 25N 10 7 E
9 Elblag, Poland ....54 10N 19 25 E
16 Elburz, Mts., Iran .....36 0N 52 0 E
28 Eldoret, Kenya......... 0 30N 35 25 E
5 Elgin, Scotland........57 39N 3 20W
39 Elizabeth, Australia....34 45S 38 35 E
35 Elizabeth, U.S.A. 40 37N 74 18W
41 Ellesmere, I., Canada ..79 30N 80 0W
1 Ellice, Is., Pacific Oc.... 8 0S 176 0 E
41 Ellsworth Land, Ant. ..75 0S 90 0W
10 Emilia Romagna, Reg.,
Italy ....44 33N 10 40 E
37 Empedrado, Argentina .28 0S 58 46W

Map
4 England, U.K. ....50 0N to 55 45 N
1 40S to 5 40W
7 English Channel, Eur. ..50 0N 2 0W
6 Ennis, Ireland 52 51N 8 59W
6 Enniscorthy, Ireland ...52 30N 6 35W
6 Enniskillen, N. Ire 54 20N 7 40W
28 Entebbe, Uganda ...... 0 3N 32 30 E
26 Enugu, Nigeria........ 6 30N 7 30 E
11 Epirus, Prov., Greece ..39 40N 20 40 E
4 Epping, England.......51 42N 0 8 E
27 Equatoria, Prov., Sud. . 5 0N 30 0 E
9 Erfurt, E. Germany....50 58N 11 2 E
35 Erie, U.S.A. 42 7N 80 2W
30 Erie, L., Can./U.S.A....42 30N 82 0W
6 Erne, L., N. Ireland....54 14N 7 30W
9 Erz Gebirge (Ore Mts.)
E. Germany ....50 25N 13 0 E
3 Erzurum, Turkey......39 57N 41 15 E
13 Esbjerg, Denmark .....55 29N 8 29 E
18 Esfahan, Iran ....32 43N 51 33 E
2 Esh Sham (Damascus),
Syria ....33 30N 36 18 E
13 Eskilstuna, Sweden ....59 22N 16 32 E
37 Esmeralda, Ecuador.... 1 0N 79 40W
38 Esperance, Australia ...33 45S 121 55 E
26 Essaouira, Morocco....31 32N 9 42W
9 Essen, Germany.......51 28N 6 59 E
37 Essequibo, R., Guyana . 5 45N 58 50W
4 Essex, co., England ....51 48N 0 30 E
9 Esslingen, Germany....48 43N 9 19 E
14 Estonia, S.S.R., U.S.S.R.58 30N 25 30 E
8 Estremadura, Prov.,
Portugal 39 0N 8 40W
18 Ethiopia, st., Africa.... 8 0N 40 0 E
10 Etna, vol., Sicily, Italy ..37 45N 15 0 E
34 Eugene, U.S.A. 44 0N 123 8W
18 Euphrates, R., Iraq ....33 30N 43 0 E
1 Europe, Continent ..36 0 N to 71 0 N
9 30W to 66 0 E
35 Evansville, U.S.A. 38 0N 87 35W
19 Everest, Mt., Nepal....28 5N 86 58 E
11 Évvoia, I., Greece .....38 30N 24 0 E
8 Évora, Portugal 38 33N 7 57W
4 Exeter, England 50 43N 3 31W
4 Exmoor, England.......51 10N 3 55W
4 Exmouth, England.....50 37N 3 24W

F

13 Fagersta, Sweden......60 1N 15 46 E
31 Fairbanks, Alaska......64 59N 147 40W
5 Falkirk, Scotland 56 0N 3 47W
1 Falkland, Is.,
Atlantic Ocean......51 30S 58 30W
1 Falkland, Is.,
Dependencies, S. Oc. 55 0S 45 0W
4 Falmouth, England 50 9N 5 5W
13 Falun, Sweden ....60 32N 15 39 E
29 Farafangana, Malagasy
Republic ....22 58S 47 57 E
18 Farasan Is., Red Sea....16 45N 41 55 E
4 Fareham, England 50 52N 1 11W
4 Farnborough, England .51 17N 0 46W
2 Faroe I.,
N. Atlantic Oc. 62 0N 7 0W
13 Farsund, Norway......58 3N 6 42W
20 Fatshan, China ....23 0N 113 4 E
4 Felixstowe, Eng. 51 58N 1 22W
14 Fergana, U.S.S.R.......40 50N 71 50 E
6 Fermanagh, co., N. Ire. 54 21N 7 40W
28 Fernando Poo, I.,
West Africa .... 3 30N 8 40 E
10 Ferrara, Italy ....44 50N 11 26 E
8 Ferrol, Spain 43 29N 8 15W
26 Fès, Morocco 34 5N 4 54W
5 Fife, co., Scotland 56 13N 3 2W
40 Fiji Is., Pacific Ocean...17 20S 179 0 E
12 Finland, Rep., Europe ..70 0N 27 0 E
4 Fishguard, Wales......51 59N 4 59W
7 Flanders, Reg., Belg....51 10N 3 15 E
13 Flekkefjord, Norway ..58 22N 6 43 E
9 Flensburg, Germany ...54 46N 9 28 E
39 Flinders Ra., Austral...31 25S 138 35 E
4 Flint, co., Wales 53 14N 3 8W
10 Florence, Italy ....43 47N 11 15 E
23 Flores, I., Indon. ...... 8 35S 121 0 E
37 Florianópólis, Brazil ...27 30S 48 30W
35 Florida, st., U.S.A. 28 30N 82 0W
10 Foggia, Italy ....41 28N 15 31 E
12 Folda, Fd., Norway ....64 43N 11 45 E
4 Folkestone, Eng. ......51 5N 1 11 E
20 Foochow, China.......26 9N 119 25 E
5 Forfar, Scotland 56 40N 2 53W
10 Forli, Italy ....44 14N 12 2 E
20 Formosa, see Taiwan
27 Fort Archambault,
Chad .... 9 5N 18 23 E
28 Fort Crampel, Cen.
Africa.............. 7 8N 19 18 E
29 Fort Dauphin, Malagasy
Rep................25 0S 46 57 E
36 Fort-de-France,
Martinique 14 36N 61 2W
27 Fort Lamy, Chad ......12 4N 15 8 E
29 Fort Victoria, Rhodesia 20 8S 30 55 E
35 Fort Wayne, U.S.A. ...41 5N 85 10W
33 Fort William, Canada ..48 20N 89 10W
5 Fort William, Scot.....56 48N 5 8W
35 Fort Worth, U.S.A. ...32 45N 97 25W
37 Fortaleza, Brazil....... 3 35S 38 35W
5 Forth, Firth of, Scot. ..56 5N 2 55W
31 Four Mountains, Is. of
the, Aleutian Is......52 50N 170 0W
31 Fox Is., Aleutian Is.....53 30N 168 0W
33 Foxe Channel, Canada .66 0N 80 0W
6 Foyle, Lough, N. Ire. ..55 6N 7 8W
7 France, Rep., Europe ..47 0N 3 0 E
28 Franceville, Gabon .... 1 40S 13 32 E
7 Franche Comté, Prov.,
France ....46 30N 5 50 E
29 Francistown, Bots. ....21 7S 27 33 E
9 Frankfurt, Germany ...50 7N 8 40 E
14 Franz Josef Land,
U.S.S.R.............80 0N 52 0 E
5 Fraserburgh, Scotland..57 41N 2 0W
13 Fredericia, Denmark...55 34N 9 43 E
13 Frederikshavn, Den....57 28N 10 31 E
13 Fredrikstad, Norway ..59 12N 10 59 E
26 Freetown, S. Leone.... 8 30N 13 10W
9 Freiburg, Germany ....48 0N 7 52 E
38 Fremantle, Australia...32 1S 115 47 E
37 French Guiana,
South America....... 4 0N 53 0W
18 Fr. Terr. of the Afars
and the Issas, Africa .11 30N 42 15 E
34 Fresno, U.S.A.........36 47N 119 50W
Frisian Is., Germany ...53 30N 6 0 E
10 Friuli Venezia Giulia,
Reg., Italy ....46 0N 13 0 E

Map
4 Frome, England 51 16N 2 17W
14 Frunze, U.S.S.R. ....42 40N 74 50 E
20 Fuchow, China........27 50N 116 14 E
21 Fujisawa, Japan ......35 25N 139 27 E
20 Fukien, Prov., China...25 50N 118 0 E
21 Fukui, Japan ....36 0N 136 10 E
21 Fukuoka, Japan ....33 30N 130 30 E
21 Fukushima, Japan .....37 45N 140 25 E
21 Funabashi, Japan .....35 45N 140 0 E
39 Furneaux Group, Is.,
Tasmania...........40 10S 147 50 E
9 Fürth, Germany.......49 29N 11 0 E
20 Fushun, China ....41 55N 123 55 E
20 Fusin, China ....42 8N 121 39 E
13 Fyn, I., Denmark .....55 18N 10 20 E

G

29 Gaberones, Botswana ..24 45S 25 55 E
28 Gabon, st., W. Africa .. 2 0S 12 0 E
37 Galapagos Is., Pac. Oc. . 0 0 89 0W
5 Galashiels, Scotland ...55 37N 2 50W
11 Galati, Rumania ....45 27N 28 2 E
8 Galicia, Prov., Spain ...42 43N 8 0W
17 Galilee, Dist., Israel ...32 53N 35 18 E
12 Gällivare, Sweden .....67 7N 20 32 E
6 Galway & co., Ireland..53 16N 9 4W
6 Galway Bay, Ireland ...53 10N 9 20W
26 Gambia, st., W. Afr....13 25N 16 0W
26 Gambia, R., W. Afr. ...13 20N 14 45W
19 Ganga (Ganges), R.,
India...............25 30N 82 0 E
26 Gao, Mali 16 15N 0 5W
10 Garda, L., Italy.......45 40N 10 40 E
7 Garonne, R., France ...44 45N 0 32W
35 Gary, U.S.A..........41 35N 87 20 E
7 Gascogne, Prov., Fr. ...43 45N 0 20 E
4 Gateshead, England....54 57N 1 37W
13 Gävle, Sweden........60 41N 17 13 E
39 Gawler, Australia .....34 30S 138 42 E
19 Gaya, India ....24 47N 85 4 E
9 Gdansk, Poland ....54 22N 18 40 E
9 Gdynia & Bay, Poland ..54 35N 18 33 E
39 Geelong, Australia ....38 2S 144 20 E
10 Geneva, tn. & L.,
Switzerland ....46 12N 6 9 E
7 Genk, Belgium........50 58N 5 32 E
10 Genoa (Genova), Italy .44 24N 8 57 E
7 Gent, Belgium ....51 4N 3 44 E
37 Georgetown, Guyana .. 6 50N 58 12W
22 Georgetown, Malaysia . 5 25N 100 19 E
14 Georgia, S.S.R.,
U.S.S.R.............41 0N 45 0 E
35 Georgia, st., U.S.A.....32 30N 82 0W
9 Gera, E. Germany.....50 53N 12 5 E
38 Geraldtown, Austral...28 48S 114 32 E
9 Germany, E.,
(Ger. Democratic Rep.)
Rep., Europe ....52 10N 12 30 E
9 Germany, W., Rep., Eur.
51 0N 10 0 E
29 Germiston, S. Africa...26 11S 28 10 E
8 Gerona, Spain ....41 58N 2 46 E
26 Ghana, st., W. Africa .. 6 0N 1 0W
17 Ghazzah, Egypt ....31 30N 34 28 E
8 Gibraltar, Europe 36 7N 5 22W
8 Gilbraltar, Str. of, Eur. 35 55N 5 40W
38 Gibson Des., Austral...24 0S 125 0 E
9 Giessen, Germany.....50 34N 8 40 E
21 Gifu, Japan ....35 30N 136 45 E
8 Gijón, Spain 43 32N 5 42W
1 Gilbert Is., Pacific Oc. . 1 0S 176 0 E
19 Gilgit, Kashmir ....35 50N 74 15 E
4 Gillingham, England ...51 23N 0 34 E
40 Gisborne, N.Z. ....38 39S 178 5 E
28 Gisenyi, Rwanda ...... 1 41S 29 30 E
15 Gizhiga, U.S.S.R. ......62 0N 150 27 E
4 Glamorgan, co., Wales.51 37N 3 35W
5 Glasgow, Scotland.....55 52N 4 14W
34 Glendale, U.S.A. 34 7N 118 18W
9 Gliwice, Poland ....50 22N 18 41 E
4 Gloucester & co., Eng..51 52N 2 15W
19 Goa, India ....15 33N 73 59 E
20 Gobi (Shamo) Desert,
Mongolia...........43 40N 109 0 E
22 Gôcông, S. Vietnam ...10 20N 107 0 E
19 Godavari, R., India ....19 5N 79 0 E
37 Goiânia, Brazil 16 35S 49 20W
14 Gomel, U.S.S.R........52 28N 31 0 E
29 Good Hope, C. of,
South Africa........34 24S 18 30 E
33 Goose Bay, Canada 53 15N 60 20W
14 Gorki, U.S.S.R. ....54 12N 31 5 E
9 Gorlitz, Germany .....51 10N 14 59 E
14 Gorlovka, U.S.S.R.....48 25N 37 58 E
4 Gosport, Eng. 50 48N 1 8W
13 Göteborg, Sweden .....57 43N 11 59 E
13 Gotland, I., Sweden ...58 15N 18 30 E
21 Goto Is., Japan........32 55N 129 10 E
37 Goya, Argentina 29 10S 59 10W
14 Graham Bell I., U.S.S.R.80 50N 63 0 E
41 Graham Land, Ant......67 0S 65 0W
29 Grahamstown, S. Afr....33 19S 26 31 E
5 Grampian Mts., Scot. ..56 50N 4 0W
36 Grand Bahama I., W. I. 26 5N 78 0W
34 Grand Canyon, U.S.A. .36 20N 113 0W
35 Grand Rapids, U.S.A. ..42 57N 85 40W
36 Granada, Nicaragua....11 58N 86 0W
8 Granada, Spain........37 10N 33 5W
8 Granada, Prov., Spain ..37 0N 3 0W
32 Grande Prairie, Can....55 15N 118 50W
5 Grangemouth, Scot....56 1N 3 43W
9 Graz, Austria ....47 4N 15 27 E
36 Great Abaco I.,
Bahamas...........26 30N 77 20W
38 Great Australian Bight,
Australia ....33 0S 130 0 E
39 Great Barrier Reef,
Australia ....19 0S 149 0 E
32 Gt. Bear, L., Canada ...65 0N 120 0W
39 Great Divide, Austral. .23 0S 146 0 E
34 Great Falls, U.S.A.....47 29N 111 19W
34 Great Salt Lake, U.S.A. 41 0N 112 30W
38 Great Sandy Desert,
Australia ....21 0S 124 0 E
32 Great Slave, L., Can....61 30N 114 20W
38 Great Victoria Desert,
Australia...........28 30S 125 0 E
20 Great Wall, China.....38 30N 109 30 E
4 Great Yarmouth, Eng. .52 40N 1 45 E
36 Greater Antilles, W. I. .17 40N 74 0W
22 Greater Sunda Is.,
Indon.............95 0 E to 125 0 E
11 Greece, King., Eur ....40 0N 23 0 E
1 Greenland, N. America 66 0N 45 0W
5 Greenock, Scotland....55 57N 4 46W
35 Greensboro, U.S.A. ...36 5N 79 47W
4 Greenwich, England ...51 28N 0 0

Map	Place	Lat.	Long.
36	Grenada, I., W. Indies	12 10N	61 40W
7	Grenoble, France	45 12N	5 42 E
40	Greymouth, N.Z.	42 29S	171 13 E
4	Grimsby, England	53 35N	0 5W
13	Grimstad, Norway	58 22N	8 35 E
7	Groningen, Neth.	53 15N	6 35 E
29	Grootfontein, S.W. Africa	19 35S	18 6 E
14	Groznyy, U.S.S.R.	43 20N	45 45 E
9	Grudziadz, Poland	53 30N	18 47 E
31	Guadalajara, Mexico	20 40N	103 20W
8	Guadalajara, Spain	40 37N	3 12W
30	Guadalupe, I., Pacific Ocean	24 20N	108 50W
36	Guadeloupe, I., French West Indies	16 20N	61 40W
8	Guadiana, R., Spain	37 55N	7 39W
8	Guadix, Spain	37 18N	3 11W
36	Guantánamó, Cuba	20 10N	75 20W
37	Guapore, R., S. Amer.	13 0S	63 0W
31	Guatemala, Rep., Central America	15 40N	90 30W
31	Guatemala, Guatemala	14 40N	90 30W
37	Guayaquil, Ecuador	2 15N	79 52W
7	Guernsey, I., Br. Isles	49 30N	2 35W
4	Guildford, England	51 14N	0 34W
26	Guinea, st., W. Afr.	10 20N	10 0W
19	Gujarat, st., India	23 20N	71 0 E
14	Guryev, U.S.S.R.	47 5N	52 0 E
37	Guyana, Rep., S. Amer.	5 0N	59 0W
7	Guyenne, Prov., France	44 30N	0 40 E
29	Gwelo, Rhodesia	19 28S	29 45 E
9	Györ, Hungary	47 41N	17 40 E

H

Map	Place	Lat.	Long.
7	Haarlem, Netherlands	52 23N	4 39 E
21	Hachinohe, Japan	40 30N	141 29 E
17	Hadera, Israel	32 27N	34 55 E
13	Haderslev, Denmark	55 17N	9 30 E
4	Hadrians Wall, Eng.	55 0N	2 30W
21	Haeju, N. Korea	38 12N	125 41 E
9	Hagen, Germany	51 21N	7 29 E
13	Hagfors, Sweden	60 3N	13 45 E
17	Haifa, Israel	32 48N	35 0 E
20	Hailar, China	49 10N	119 50 E
20	Hainan, I., China	19 10N	109 30 E
22	Haiphong, N. Vietnam	20 45S	106 35 E
36	Haiti, Rep., Hispaniola, I., W. Indies	19 6N	72 30W
2	Halab, (Aleppo), Syria	36 12N	37 13 E
33	Halifax, Canada	44 38N	63 35W
4	Halifax, England	53 43N	1 51W
9	Halle, E. Germany	51 29N	12 0 E
23	Halmahera, I., Indon.	0 40N	128 0 E
13	Halmstad, Sweden	56 37N	12 56 E
13	Hälsingborg, Sweden	56 3N	12 42 E
16	Hamadan, Iran	34 52N	48 32 E
21	Hamamatsu, Japan	34 45N	137 45 E
13	Hamar, Norway	60 48N	11 7 E
9	Hamburg, Germany	53 32N	9 59 E
13	Hameenlinna, Finland	61 3N	24 26 E
9	Hameln, Germany	52 6N	6 10 E
21	Hamhung, N. Korea	39 54N	127 35 E
39	Hamilton, Australia	37 37S	142 0 E
36	Hamilton, Bermuda	32 16N	64 46W
33	Hamilton, Canada	43 20N	79 50W
40	Hamilton, N.Z.	37 47S	175 19 E
5	Hamilton, Scotland	55 47N	4 2W
12	Hammerfest, Norway	70 33N	23 50 E
4	Hampshire, co., Eng.	51 3N	1 20W
18	Handa, Somali Rep.	10 49N	51 5 E
20	Hangchow, China	30 20N	120 5 E
13	Hanko, Finland	59 50N	23 2 E
22	Hanoi, N. Vietnam	21 5N	105 40 E
9	Hanover, Germany	52 23N	9 43 E
12	Haparanda, Sweden	65 52N	24 8 E
20	Harbin, China	45 45N	126 41 E
18	Harer, Ethiopia	9 20N	42 8 E
18	Hargeisa, Somali Rep.	9 30N	44 2 E
4	Harlech, Wales	52 52N	4 8W
13	Härnösand, Sweden	62 38N	18 5 E
5	Harris, Dist., Scotland	57 50N	6 55W
4	Harrogate, England	53 59N	1 32W
29	Hartley, Rhodesia	18 10S	30 7 E
4	Harwich, England	51 56N	1 18 E
9	Harz Mts., Germany	51 40N	10 40 E
4	Hastings, England	50 51N	0 36 E
40	Hastings, N.Z.	39 39S	176 52 E
4	Hatfield, England	51 46N	0 13W
13	Haugesund, Norway	59 25N	5 19 E
36	Havana, Cuba	23 0N	82 30W
31	Hawaii, st., U.S.A., Pacific Ocean	20 0N	155 0W
5	Hawick, Scotland	55 25N	2 48W
4	Haywards Heath, Eng.	51 0N	0 5W
33	Hearst, Canada	49 40N	83 41W
17	Hebron, Jordan	31 32N	35 6 E
9	Heilbronn, Germany	49 8N	9 14 E
20	Heilungkiang, Prov., China	47 0N	129 0 E
9	Heligoland Bay, Ger.	54 0N	8 0 E
13	Helsingör, Denmark	56 2N	12 35 E
13	Helsinki, Finland	60 15N	25 3 E
20	Hengyang, China	26 58N	112 25 E
19	Henzada, Burma	17 38N	95 35 E
19	Herat, Afghan	34 20N	62 7 E
4	Hereford, England	52 4N	2 42W
4	Hereford, co., England	52 4N	2 43W
30	Hermosillo, Mexico	29 10N	111 0W
13	Herning, Denmark	56 8N	9 0 E
4	Hertford, co., England	51 51N	0 5W
4	High Wycombe, Eng.	51 37N	0 45W
31	Hilo, Hawaiian Is.	19 42N	155 4W
19	Himalaya, Mts., Asia	30 0N	80 0 E
19	Hindu Kush, Ra., Afghan	36 0N	71 0 E
21	Hiroshima, Japan	37 40N	132 30 E
36	Hispaniola, I.,W. Ind.	19 0N	71 0W
21	Hitachi, Japan	36 48N	140 43 E
13	Hjörring, Denmark	57 29N	9 59 E
39	Hobart, Tasmania	42 50S	147 21 E
18	Hodeida, Yemen	14 50N	43 0 E
11	Hodmezövasarhely, Hungary	46 28N	20 22 E
20	Hofei, China	31 48N	117 15 E
20	Hoihow, China	20 0N	110 20 E
21	Hokkaido, I., Japan	43 30N	143 0 E
36	Holguin, Cuba	20 50N	76 20W
13	Holstebro, Den.	56 22N	8 33 E
4	Holyhead, Wales	53 18N	4 38W
2	Homs, Syria	34 40N	36 45 E
20	Honan, Prov., China	33 45N	113 20 E
31	Honduras, Rep., Central America	14 40N	86 30W
20	Hongkong, Brit. Crown Colony, China	22 11N	14 14 E
31	Honolulu, tn & I., Hawaiian Is.	21 25N	157 55W
21	Honshu, I., Japan	36 0N	138 0 E
20	Hopei, Prov., China	39 25N	116 45 E
13	Horsens, Denmark	55 52N	9 50 E
4	Horsham, England	51 4N	0 20W
13	Horten, Norway	59 25N	10 32 E
8	Hospitalet, Spain	41 21N	2 6 E
35	Houston, U.S.A.	29 50N	95 20W
19	Howrah, India	22 37N	88 27 E
5	Hoy, I., Scotland	58 50N	3 15W
9	Hradec Králové, Pol.	50 15N	15 50 E
20	Hsinchu, Taiwan	24 48N	120 59 E
37	Huancayo, Peru	12 5S	75 0W
4	Huddersfield, England	53 38N	1 49W
33	Hudson Bay, Canada	60 0N	86 0W
22	Hue, S. Vietnam	16 60N	107 35 E
8	Huelva, Spain	37 18N	6 57W
8	Huesca, Spain	42 8N	0 25W
20	Huhehot, China	40 50N	116 50 E
4	Hull, England	53 45N	0 20W
4	Humber, R., England	53 42N	0 20W
20	Hunan, Prov., China	27 35N	111 20 E
2	Hungary, st., Europe	47 20N	19 20 E
21	Hungnam, N. Korea	40 0N	127 30 E
4	Huntingdon & Peterborough, co., England	52 23N	0 10W
20	Hupei, Prov., China	31 5N	113 5 E
30	Huron, L., Can./U.S.A.	45 0N	83 0W
12	Husavik, Iceland	66 3N	17 13W
10	Hvar, I., Y.-Slav.	43 11N	16 28 E
20	Hwainan, China	32 31N	116 58 E
20	Hwangshih, China	30 8N	115 0 E
19	Hyderabad, India	17 10N	78 20 E
19	Hyderabad, W. Pak.	25 23N	68 36 E

I

Map	Place	Lat.	Long.
11	Iasi, Rumania	47 10N	27 40 E
26	Ibadan, Nigeria	7 22N	3 58 E
8	Ibiza, I., Spain	39 0N	1 30 E
29	Ibo, Mozambique	12 21S	40 40 E
12	Iceland, Rep., Europe	65 0N	19 0W
34	Idaho, st., U.S.A.	44 10N	114 0W
26	Ife, Nigeria	7 30N	4 31 E
7	IJsselmeer, Neth.	52 45N	5 20 E
11	Ikaria, I., Greece	37 35N	26 10 E
7	Ile de France, Prov., France	49 0N	2 20 E
4	Ilkeston, England	52 59N	1 19W
35	Illinois, st., U.S.A.	40 15N	89 30W
23	Iloilo, Philippines	10 45N	122 33 E
19	Imphal, India	24 15N	94 0 E
11	Imroz, I., Turkey	40 10N	26 0 E
12	Inari, L., Finland	69 0N	28 0 E
21	Inchon, S. Korea	37 30N	126 30 E
19	India, st., Asia	23 0N	80 0 E
35	Indiana, st., U.S.A.	40 0N	86 0W
35	Indianapolis, U.S.A.	39 42N	86 10W
22	Indonesia, Rep., Asia	5 0S	115 0 E
19	Indore, India	22 42N	75 53 E
19	Indus, R., W. Pakistan	28 40N	70 10 E
29	Inhambane, Mozam.	23 51S	35 29 E
21	Inland Sea, Japan	34 30N	133 30 E
20	Inner Mongolia, Autonomous Region, China	45 0N	120 0 E
9	Innsbruck, Austria	47 16N	11 23 E
40	Invercargill, N.Z.	46 24S	168 24 E
5	Inverness, Scotland	57 29N	4 12W
5	Inverness, co., Scot.	57 7N	4 35W
11	Ionian, Is., Greece	38 40N	20 0 E
11	Ionian Sea, Europe	37 30N	17 30 E
35	Iowa, st., U.S.A.	42 18N	93 30W
22	Ipoh, Malaysia	4 36N	101 4 E
4	Ipswich, England	52 4N	1 9 E
37	Iquique, Chile	20 19S	70 5W
37	Iquitos, Peru	3 45S	73 10W
10	Iraklion (Candia) Gr.	35 20N	25 12 E
16	Iran (Persia), st., Asia	33 0N	53 0 E
16	Iraq, st., Asia	33 0N	44 0 E
28	Irebu, Congo	0 40S	17 55 E
6	Ireland, Rep., Europe	53 0N	8 0W
4	Irish Sea, Europe	54 0N	5 0W
15	Irkutsk, U.S.S.R.	52 10N	104 20 E
19	Irrawaddy, R., Burma	19 30N	95 15 E
28	Irumu, Congo	1 22N	29 55 E
12	Isafjördur, Iceland	66 10N	23 15W
5	Islay, I., Scotland	55 46N	6 10W
4	Isle of Man, Brit. Is.	54 30N	4 40W
4	Isle of Wight, England	50 40N	1 20W
27	Ismailia, Egypt	30 37N	32 18 E
17	Israel, st., Asia	32 30N	32 30 E
11	Istanbul, Turkey	41 0N	29 0 E
10	Istra, Dist., Y.-Slav.	45 20N	14 0 E
10	Italy, Rep., Europe	42 0N	13 0 E
14	Ivanovo, U.S.S.R.	57 5N	41 0 E
26	Ivory Coast, st., W. Africa	7 30N	5 0W
14	Izhevsk, U.S.S.R.	56 50N	53 0 E
2	Izmir, Turkey	38 25N	27 8 E

J

Map	Place	Lat.	Long.
18	Jabal al Tuwaiq, Saudi Arabia	24 0N	45 50 E
19	Jabalpur, India	23 9N	79 58 E
35	Jackson, U.S.A.	32 20N	90 10W
35	Jacksonville, U.S.A.	30 15N	81 38W
8	Jaen, Spain	37 44N	3 43W
19	Jaffna, Ceylon	9 45S	80 2 E
19	Jaipur, India	20 51N	86 28 E
36	Jamaica, I., W. Indies	18 10N	77 30W
19	Jammu & Kashmir, st., Asia	32 44N	74 54 E
19	Jamnagar, India	22 30N	70 0 E
19	Jamshedpur, India	22 44N	86 20 E
21	Japan, st., Asia	36 0N	136 0 E
17	Japan, Sea of, Asia	40 0N	135 0 E
4	Jarrow, England	54 58N	1 28W
37	Jau, Brazil	22 10S	48 30W
22	Java, I., Indonesia	7 0S	110 0 E
9	Jena, E. Germany	50 56N	11 33 E
17	Jenin, Jordan	32 28N	35 18 E
8	Jerez, Spain	36 41N	6 7W
17	Jericho, Jordan	31 52N	35 27 E
7	Jersey, I., Br. Isles	49 13N	2 7W
35	Jersey City, U.S.A.	40 41N	74 8W
17	Jerusalem, Israel	31 47N	35 10 E
19	Jhansi, India	25 30N	78 36 E
18	Jidda, Saudi Arabia	21 29N	39 16 E
18	Jima, Ethiopia	7 40N	36 55 E
37	João Pessoa, Brazil	7 10S	35 0W
19	Jodhpur, India	26 23N	73 2 E
22	Jogjakarta, Java	6 9S	106 49 E
29	Johannesburg, S. Afr.	26 10N	28 8 E
5	John O'Groats, Scot.	58 39N	3 3W
22	Johore Bahru, Malaysia.	1 28N	103 46 E
37	Joinville, Brazil	26 15S	48 55 E
13	Jonköping, Sweden	57 45N	14 10 E
18	Jordan, st., Asia	31 0N	36 0 E
17	Jordan, R., Isr./Jordan	32 10N	35 32 E
27	Juba, Sudan	4 57N	31 35 E
25	Juba, R., E. Africa	1 30N	42 35 E
17	Judea, Wilderness of, Israel/Jordan	31 30N	35 15 E
37	Juiz de Fora, Brazil	21 43S	43 19W
19	Jullundur, India	31 20N	75 40 E
31	Juneau, Alaska	58 21N	134 20W
5	Jura I., Scotland	56 0N	5 50W
13	Jyväskylä, Finland	62 12N	25 47 E

K

Map	Place	Lat.	Long.
26	Kabala, Sierra Leone	9 38N	11 37W
19	Kabul, Afghan	34 28N	69 18 E
19	Kabul, R., Afghan	34 30N	70 0 E
29	Kabwe (Broken Hill), Zambia	14 27S	28 28 E
26	Kaduna, Nigeria	10 30N	7 21 E
21	Kaesong, N. Korea	38 1N	126 46 E
18	Kaf, Saudi Arabia	31 22N	37 25 E
26	Kafanchan, Nigeria	9 40N	8 20 E
21	Kagoshima, Japan	31 36N	130 40 E
20	Kaifeng, China	34 45N	114 30 E
31	Kailua Laniki, Hawaii	21 33N	157 45W
12	Kajaani, Finland	64 17N	27 46 E
29	Kalahari, Desert, Botswana	24 0S	22 0 E
20	Kalgan, China	40 50N	114 50 E
38	Kalgoorlie, Australia	30 40S	121 22 E
23	Kalimantan, Prov., Indonesia	0 1S	115 0 E
14	Kalinin, U.S.S.R.	56 55N	35 55 E
13	Kaliningrad, U.S.S.R.	54 42N	20 32 E
9	Kalisz, Poland	51 45N	18 8 E
13	Kalmar, Sweden	56 39N	16 22 E
14	Kalmyk, A.S.S.R., U.S.S.R.	46 0N	47 0 E
14	Kaluga, U.S.S.R.	54 35N	36 10 E
18	Kamaran I., Red Sea	15 28N	42 35 E
15	Kamchatka Pen., U.S.S.R.	57 0N	160 0 E
28	Kampala, Uganda	0 20N	32 30 E
22	Kampar, Malaysia	4 18N	101 9 E
21	Kanazawa, Japan	36 30N	136 38 E
19	Kandahar, Afghan	31 32N	65 30 E
19	Kandy, Ceylon	7 18N	80 43 E
31	Kaneohe, Hawaiian Is.	21 25N	157 48W
26	Kankan, Guinea	10 30N	9 15W
26	Kano, Nigeria	12 0N	8 30 E
19	Kanpur, India	26 35N	80 20 E
34	Kansas, st., U.S.A.	38 30N	98 0W
35	Kansas City, Kansas, U.S.A.	39 0N	94 37W
35	Kansas City, Mo., U.S.A.	39 4N	94 31 E
20	Kansu, Prov., China	36 5N	105 30 E
29	Kanye, Botswana	24 59S	25 19 E
20	Kaoksiung, Taiwan	22 35N	120 16 E
14	Kara Bogaz Gol, U.S.S.R.	41 0N	53 30 E
14	Kara Sea, U.S.S.R.	75 0N	70 0 E
19	Karachi, W. Pakistan	24 53N	67 0 E
14	Karaganda, U.S.S.R.	49 50N	73 0 E
19	Karakoram Ra, India	35 20N	78 0 E
18	Karbala, Iraq	32 47N	44 3 E
14	Karelian, A.S.S.R., U.S.S.R.	63 0N	32 30 E
29	Kariba, L., Zam./Rhod.	16 40S	28 20 E
9	Karl Marx Stadt (Chemnitz), E. Ger.	50 50N	12 55 E
13	Karlshamn, Sweden	56 13N	14 56 E
13	Karlskrona, Sweden	56 12N	15 42 E
9	Karlsruhe, Germany	49 3N	8 23 E
13	Karlstad, Sweden	59 24N	13 35 E
19	Karnaphuli Res., E. Pakistan	22 45N	92 15 E
10	Karpathos, I., Greece	35 47N	27 10 E
14	Karsakpai, U.S.S.R.	47 55N	66 40 E
28	Kasanga, Tanzamia	8 29S	31 9 E
29	Kasempa, Zambia	13 30S	25 48 E
20	Kashgar, China	39 30N	76 10 E
27	Kassala, Sudan	15 23N	36 26 E
9	Kassel, Germany	15 19N	9 32 E
19	Katmandu, Nepal	27 45N	85 12 E
26	Katsina, Nigeria	7 10N	9 20 E
13	Kattegat, Str., Den.	56 50N	11 20 E
31	Kauai, I., Hawaiian Is.	22 0N	160 0W
14	Kaunas, U.S.S.R.	54 54N	23 54 E
21	Kawagoe, Japan	36 0N	139 30 E
21	Kawasaki, Japan	35 40N	139 45 E
26	Kayes, Mali	14 25N	11 30W
2	Kayseri, Turkey	38 45N	35 30 E
14	Kazakhstan, S.S.R., U.S.S.R.	49 0N	50 0 E
14	Kazan, U.S.S.R.	55 48N	49 3 E
20	Keelung, Taiwan	25 3N	121 45 E
11	Kefallinia, I., Greece	38 28N	20 30 E
26	Keffi, Nigeria	8 55N	7 43 E
14	Kemerovo, U.S.S.R.	55 20N	85 50W
12	Kemi, Finland	65 48N	24 43 E
4	Kendal, England	54 19N	2 44W
26	Kenitra, Morocco	34 11N	6 30W
35	Kennedy, C., U.S.A.	28 28N	80 31W
4	Kent, co., England	51 12N	0 40 E
35	Kentucky, st., U.S.A.	37 20N	85 0W
28	Kenya, st., E. Africa	0 5N	37 0 E
19	Kerala, st., India	11 0N	76 15 E
14	Kerch, U.S.S.R.	45 20N	36 20 E
1	Kerguelen, I., Indian Ocean	48 30S	69 40 E
11	Kerkira (Corfu), I., Gr.	39 40N	19 50 E
40	Kermadec Is., Pac. Oc.	31 8S	175 16W
18	Kerman, Iran	30 15N	57 1 E
6	Kerry, co., Ireland	52 7N	9 35W
31	Ketchikan, Alaska	55 25N	131 42W
35	Key West, U.S.A.	24 40N	82 0W
15	Khabarovsk, U.S.S.R.	48 20N	135 0 E
17	Khan Yunis, Egypt	31 21N	34 18 E
14	Kharkov, U.S.S.R.	49 58N	36 20 E
27	Khartoum, Sudan	15 31N	32 35 E
11	Khios, I., Greece	38 23N	29 0 E
19	Khyber P., Afghan	34 10N	71 8 E
20	Kiamusze, China	46 45N	130 30 E
20	Kiangsi, Prov., China	27 30N	115 0 E
20	Kiangsu, Prov., China	33 15N	119 30 E
9	Kiel, Germany	54 16N	10 8 E
14	Kiev, U.S.S.R.	50 30N	30 28 E
26	Kiffa, Mauritania	16 50N	11 15W
11	Kikládhes (Cyclades) Is. Greece	37 50N	25 0 E
6	Kildare, co., Ireland	53 10N	6 50W
25	Kilimanjaro, Mt., Kenya	3 4S	37 21 E
6	Kilkenny & co., Ireland	52 40N	7 17W
6	Killarney, Ireland	52 2N	9 30W
5	Kilmarnock, Scotland	55 36N	4 30W
29	Kilwa Kivinje, Tanz.	8 45S	39 25 E
29	Kimberley, S. Africa	28 43N	24 46 E
38	Kimberley, Dist., Australia	16 20S	126 0 E
5	Kincardine, Scotland	57 52N	4 20W
28	Kindu, Congo	2 53S	25 57 E
39	King, I., Tasmania, Australia	39 40S	144 0 E
4	King's Lynn, England	52 45N	0 25 E
36	Kingston, Jamaica	18 0N	76 50W
5	Kinross, co., Scotland	56 10N	3 30W
28	Kinshasa, Congo	4 20N	15 15 E
5	Kintyre, Dist., Scot.	55 32N	5 35W
15	Kirensk, U.S.S.R.	57 50N	107 55 E
14	Kirgizia, S.S.R., U.S.S.R.	42 0N	75 0 E
20	Kirin, China	43 50N	126 38 E
20	Kirin, Prov., China	43 45N	125 20 E
5	Kirkcaldy, Scotland	56 7N	3 10W
5	Kirkcudbright, Scot.	54 50N	4 3W
5	Kirkcudbright, co., Scotland	55 2N	4 5W
5	Kirkwall, Orkney, Scotland	58 59N	2 59W
14	Kirov, U.S.S.R.	58 25N	49 40 E
14	Kirovabad, U.S.S.R.	40 45N	46 10 E
14	Kirovograd, U.S.S.R.	48 35N	32 20 E
12	Kiruna, Sweden	67 50N	20 20 E
21	Kiryu, Japan	36 34N	139 12 E
28	Kisangani, Congo	0 41N	25 11 E
14	Kishinev, U.S.S.R.	47 1N	28 50 E
25	Kismayu, Somali Rep.	0 20S	42 30 E
26	Kissidougou, Guinea	9 5N	10 0W
28	Kisumu, Kenya	0 3S	34 57 E
21	Kitakyushu, Japan	33 50N	130 50 E
28	Kitale, Kenya	1 0N	35 12 E
33	Kitchener, Canada	43 30N	80 30W
28	Kitega, Burundi,	3 30S	29 58 E
10	Kithira, I., Greece	36 18N	23 0 E
29	Kitwe, Zambia	12 50S	28 0 E
9	Klagenfurt, Austria	46 38N	14 20 E
22	Klang, Malaysia	3 3N	101 27 E
32	Klondike, Dist., Can.	64 0N	139 40W
22	Kluang, Malaysia	2 1N	103 20 E
35	Knoxville, U.S.A.	35 58N	83 57W
21	Kobe, Japan	34 45N	135 10 E
9	Koblenz, Germany	50 21N	7 36 E
21	Kochi, Japan	33 30N	133 35 E
31	Kodiak, I., Alaska	57 30N	153 30W
21	Kofu, Japan	35 40N	138 30 E
13	Köge, Denmark	55 27N	12 10 E
14	Kokand, U.S.S.R.	41 0N	71 10 E
20	Kokiu, China	23 25N	103 5 E
13	Kokkola, Finland	63 50N	23 8 E
19	Kolar, India	13 12N	78 15 E
19	Kolhapur, India	16 43N	74 15 E
15	Komandorskiye Is., U.S.S.R.	55 0N	167 0 E
14	Komi, A.S.S.R., U.S.S.R.	64 0N	55 0 E
15	Komsomolsk, U.S.S.R.	50 30N	137 0 E
41	Komsomolskaya, Ant.	73 45S	97 0 E
13	Kongsberg, Norway	59 37N	9 38 E
9	Konstanz, Germany	47 39N	9 10 E
2	Konya, Turkey	37 52N	32 35 E
12	Kópavogur, Iceland	64 10N	21 50W
13	Kopervik, Norway	59 17N	5 20 E
10	Korčula, I., Y. Slav.	42 57N	16 55 E
21	Korea Str., Korea/ Japan	28 40N	134 10 E
26	Korhogo, Ivory Coast	9 29N	5 28W
13	Korsör, Denmark	55 20N	11 9 E
11	Kos, I., Greece	36 50N	27 10 E
39	Kosciusko, Mt., Australia	36 27S	148 16 E
2	Kosice, Cz.	48 42N	21 15 E
27	Kosti, Sudan	13 8N	32 43 E
22	Kota Bharu, Malaysia	6 7N	102 14 E
23	Kota Kinabalu (Jesselton) Malaysia	6 0N	116 12 E
13	Kotka, Finland	60 29N	27 0 E
20	Kowloon, Hongkong	22 25N	114 10 E
19	Kozhikode, India	11 15N	75 43 E
13	Kragerö, Norway	58 56N	9 30 E
2	Kraków, Poland	50 3N	19 55 E
13	Kramfors, Sweden	62 55N	17 48 E
14	Krasnodar, U.S.S.R.	45 5N	38 50 E
14	Krasnovodsk, U.S.S.R.	50 0N	52 52 E
15	Krasnoyarsk, U.S.S.R.	56 8N	93 0 E
9	Krefeld, Germany	51 20N	6 22 E
28	Kribi, Cameroon	2 57N	9 56 E
19	Krishna, R., India	16 26N	76 45 E
13	Kristiansund, Norway	63 10N	7 45 E
13	Kristinstad see Kristiinankaupunki		
13	Kristiinankaupunki, Finland	62 18N	21 25 E
14	Krivoy Rog, U.S.S.R.	47 51N	33 20 E
10	Krk, I., Y. Slav.	45 5N	14 56 E
29	Krugersdorp, S. Afr.	26 5S	27 46 E
22	Kuala Dungun, Malaysia	4 46N	103 25 E
22	Kuala Lumpur, Malaysia	3 9N	101 41 E
22	Kuala Trengganu, Malaysia	5 20N	103 8 E
22	Kuantan, Malaysia	3 49N	103 20 E
22	Kuching, Sarawak, Malaysia	1 33N	110 25 E
20	Kuldja, China	44 0N	81 0 E
21	Kumamoto, Japan	32 45N	130 45 E
26	Kumasi, Ghana	6 41N	1 38W
21	Kunsan, S. Korea	35 59N	126 45 E
20	Kunming, China	25 0N	102 45 E
13	Kuopio, Finland	62 53N	27 35 E
21	Kure, Japan	33 15N	133 15 E
14	Kurgan, U.S.S.R.	55 30N	65 0 E
15	Kuril Is., U.S.S.R.	45 0N	150 0 E
14	Kursk, U.S.S.R.	51 42N	36 11 E
21	Kurume, Japan	33 15N	130 30 E
21	Kushiro, Japan	43 0N	144 30 E
18	Kuwait, st., Asia	29 30N	47 30 E
14	Kuybyshev, U.S.S.R.	53 20N	57 0 E
21	Kwangju, S. Korea	35 10N	126 45 E
21	Kwangnung, S. Korea	37 50N	128 56 E
20	Kwangsi Chuang, Autonomous Region, China	23 0N	109 0 E
20	Kwangtung, Prov., China	23 35N	114 0 E
20	Kweichow, Prov., China	26 40N	107 0 E
20	Kweilin, China	25 16N	110 15 E
20	Kweiyang, China	26 30N	106 35 E
21	Kyoto, Japan	35 0N	135 45 E
21	Kyushu, I., Japan	32 30N	131 0 E
14	Kzyl Orda, U.S.S.R.	44 50N	65 10 E

L

Map	Place	Lat.	Long.
10	L'Aquila, Italy	42 26N	13 24 E
36	La Ceiba, Honduras	15 40N	86 50W
8	La Coruña, Spain	43 20N	8 25W
37	La Guaira, Venezuela	10 40N	67 0W
8	La Linea, Spain	36 15N	5 23W
37	La Paz, Bolivia	16 20S	68 10W
37	La Plata, Argentine	35 0S	57 55W
37	La Plata, Rio de, Uruguay/Argentine	35 0S	56 40W
7	La Rochelle, France	46 10N	1 9W
37	La Serena, Chile	29 55S	71 10W
10	La Spezia, Italy	44 8N	9 48 E
36	La Vega, Dominican Rep.	19 20N	70 30W
33	Labrador, Reg., Can.	53 20N	61 0W
19	Laccadive Is., Indian Oc.	10 0N	72 30 E
14	Ladoga, L., U.S.S.R.	61 15N	30 30 E
29	Ladysmith, S. Afr.	28 32S	29 46 E
13	Læsö, I., Denmark	57 15N	10 53 E
6	Lagan, R., N. Ireland	54 35N	5 55W
26	Lagos, Nigeria	6 25N	3 27 E
8	Lagos, Portugal	37 5N	8 41W
19	Lahore, W. Pakistan	31 32N	74 22 E
13	Lahti, Finland	60 59N	25 45 E
25	Lamu, Kenya	2 10S	40 58 E
31	Lanai, I., Hawaiian Is.	20 50N	156 55W
5	Lanark & co., Scotland	55 40N	3 48W
4	Lancashire, co., England	53 40N	2 30W
4	Lancaster, England	54 3N	2 48W
20	Lanchow, China	36 0N	103 50 E
4	Land's End, England	50 4N	5 43W
7	Languedoc, Prov., France	43 58N	3 22 E
35	Lansing, U.S.A.	42 47N	84 32W
6	Laois, co., Ireland	53 0N	7 20W
22	Laos, st., Asia	17 45N	105 0 E
12	Lapland, Reg., Sweden & Finland	68 0N	26 0 E
15	Laptev Sea, U.S.S.R.	76 0N	125 0 E
34	Laredo, U.S.A.	27 34N	99 29W
5	Largs, Scotland	55 48N	4 51W
11	Lárisa, Greece	39 38N	22 28 E
6	Larne, N. Ireland	54 52N	5 50W
26	Las Palmas, Canary Is.	28 10N	15 28W
19	Lashio, Burma	23 0N	98 0 E
10	Latium, Reg., Italy	42 0N	12 30 E
14	Latvia, S.S.R., U.S.S.R.	56 45N	24 30 E
4	Launceston, England	50 38N	4 21W
39	Launceston, Tasmania, Australia	41 24S	147 8 E
10	Lausanne, Switzerland	46 32N	6 38 E
23	Laut, I., Indonesia	3 40S	116 10 E
7	Le Havre, France	49 30N	0 5 E
7	Le Mans, France	48 0N	0 12 E
4	Leamington, England	52 18N	1 32W
2	Lebanon, st., Asia	34 0N	36 0 E
10	Lecce, Italy	40 20N	18 10 E
4	Leeds, England	53 48N	1 34W
36	Leeward Is., W. Indies	16 30N	63 30W
23	Legaspi, Philippines	13 10N	123 46 E
10	Leghorn, Italy	43 32N	10 18 E
9	Legnica, Poland	51 12N	16 10 E
29	Lehututu, Botswana	24 0S	22 0 E
4	Leicester & co., Eng.	52 39N	1 9W
6	Leinster, Prov., Ireland	53 0N	7 10W
9	Leipzig, E. Germany	51 20N	12 23 E
5	Leith, Scotland	55 55N	3 11W
6	Leitrim, co., Ireland	54 8N	8 0W
15	Lena, R., U.S.S.R.	64 30N	127 0 E
14	Leningrad, U.S.S.R.	59 55N	30 20 E
4	Leominster, England	52 15N	2 43W
31	León, Mexico	21 7N	101 30W
36	Léon, Nicaragua	12 20N	86 51W
8	León, Spain	42 38N	5 34W
8	Leon, Prov., Spain	41 40N	5 55W
8	Lérida, Spain	41 37N	0 39 E
5	Lerwick, Zetland, Scotland	60 10N	1 10W
36	Les Cayes, Haiti	18 15N	73 46W
29	Lesotho, st., S. Africa	29 40S	28 0 E
36	Lesser Antilles, W. Indies	12 30N	61 0W
23	Lesser Sunda Is., Indon.	7 30S	120 0 E
11	Lésvos, I., Greece	26 0N	39 15 E
32	Lethbridge, Canada	49 45N	112 45W
6	Letterkenney, Ireland	54 57N	7 42W
11	Levkás, I., Greece	38 40N	20 43 E
5	Lewis, Dist., Scotland	58 10N	6 40W
23	Leyte, I., Philippines	10 45N	125 5 E
20	Lhasa, Tibet, China	29 40N	91 10 E
20	Liaoning, Prov., China	41 40N	122 30 E
20	Liaoyang, China	41 15N	123 10 E
20	Liaoyuan, China	42 51N	125 12 E
9	Liberec, Cz.	50 47N	15 7 E
36	Liberia, Costa Rica	10 40N	85 30W
26	Liberia, st., W. Africa	6 30N	9 30W
28	Libreville, Gabon	0 25N	9 26 E
27	Libya, st., N. Africa	28 30N	17 30 E
13	Lidköping, Sweden	58 31N	13 14 E
9	Liechtenstein, Principality, Europe	47 8N	9 35 E
7	Liége, Belgium	50 38N	5 35 E
6	Liffey, R., Ireland	53 21N	6 20W
10	Liguria, Reg., Italy	44 20N	8 30 E
10	Ligurian Sea, Europe	43 20N	9 0 E
29	Likasa (Jadotville), Congo	10 55S	26 48 E
7	Lille, France	50 38N	3 3 E
29	Lilongwe, Malawi	14 0S	33 48 E
37	Lima, Peru	12 0S	77 0W
2	Limassol, Cyprus	34 42N	33 1 E
6	Limerick & co., Ireland	52 40N	8 38W
11	Limnos, I., Greece	39 50N	25 15 E
7	Limoges, France	45 50N	1 15 E
7	Limousin, Prov., France	45 30N	1 40 E
29	Limpopo, R. Africa	24 15S	32 45 E
37	Linares Chile	35 50S	71 40W
8	Linares, Spain	38 10N	3 40W
4	Lincoln, England	53 14N	0 32W
35	Lincoln, U.S.A.	40 50N	96 42W
4	Lincoln, co., England	53 11N	0 20W
13	Linköping, Sweden	58 28N	15 36 E
20	Linsia, China	35 31N	108 8 E
9	Linz, Austria	48 18N	14 18 E
7	Lion, Golfe du, France	43 0N	4 0W
10	Lipari, Is., Italy	38 40N	15 0 E
28	Lisala, Congo	2 12N	21 38 E
8	Lisbon (Lisboa), Port.	38 42N	9 10W
6	Lisburn, N. Ireland	54 30N	6 2W
14	Lithuania, S.S.R., U.S.S.R.	55 30N	24 0 E
35	Little Rock, U.S.A.	34 41N	92 10W
20	Liuchow, China	24 10N	109 10 E
4	Liverpool, England	53 25N	3 0W
29	Livingstone, Zambia	17 50N	25 50 E
29	Livingstonia, Malawi	10 38S	34 5 E
10	Ljubjana, Y. Slav.	46 4N	14 33 E
4	Llandudno, Wales	53 19N	3 51W
4	Llanelli, Wales	51 41N	4 11W
29	Lobito, Angola	12 18S	13 35 E

Map
17 Lod (Lydda), Israel ....31 57N 34 54 E
2 Lódz, Poland..........51 45N 19 27 E
12 Lofoten, I., Norway ...68 20N 14 0 E
8 Logroño, Spain........42 28N 2 32W
7 Loire, R., France 47 25N 0 20W
13 Lolland, I., Denmark...54 45N 11 30 E
10 Lombardy, Reg., Italy..45 33N 9 40 E
23 Lombok, I., Indon...... 8 35S 116 20 E
26 Lome, Togo .... 6 9N 1 20 E
5 Lomond, L., Scotland ..56 8N 4 38W
13 Lomza, Poland ....53 10N 22 2 E
33 London, Canada.......43 0N 81 15W
4 London, England 51 30N 0 5W
6 Londonderry & co., N. Ireland..........55 0N 7 20W
34 Long Beach, U.S.A.....33 46N 118 12W
34 Long Island, U.S.A.....40 50N 73 20W
22 Long Xuyen, S. Vietnam ....10 19N 105 28 E
6 Longford & co., Ireland 53 43N 7 50W
8 Lorca, Spain 37 41N 1 42W
5 Lorn, Firth of, Scot. ...56 20N 5 40W
7 Lorraine, Prov., France 49 0N 6 0 E
34 Los Angeles, U.S.A. ...34 0N 118 10W
36 Los Hermanos, I., Venezuela..........11 50N 64 20W
10 Lošinj, I., Y. Slav.......44 55N 14 45 E
4 Loughborough, Eng. ..52 46N 1 11W
1 Louisiade Arch., Pacific Ocean ....10 50S 152 30 E
35 Louisiana, st., U.S.A....30 50N 92 0W
35 Louisville, U.S.A.......38 15N 85 45W
7 Lourdes, France.......43 6N 0 3W
29 Lourenço Marques, Mozam.............25 57N 32 34 E
6 Louth, co., Ireland.....53 55N 6 30W
30 Lower California, Pen., Mexico.............28 0N 112 30W
40 Lower Hutt, N.Z......41 10S 174 55 E
9 Lower Saxony, Land, Germany...........52 47N 91 5 E
4 Lowestoft, England ....52 29N 1 44 E
20 Loyang, China ....34 40N 112 28 E
20 Lü-ta, China...........39 0N 121 31 E
29 Luanda, Angola .... 8 58S 13 9 E
22 Luang Prabang, Laos ...19 45N 102 10 E
29 Luanshya, Zambia .....13 20S 28 8 E
34 Lubbock, U.S.A. 33 40N 102 0W
9 Lubeck, Germany .....53 52N 10 41 E
2 Lublin, Poland ....51 12N 22 38 E
29 Lubumbashi, Congo ...11 32S 27 28 E
10 Lucca, Italy ....43 50N 10 30 E
20 Luchow, China.........28 54N 105 17 E
19 Lucknow, India ....26 50N 81 0 E
29 Lüderitz, S.W. Africa ..26 37S 15 9 E
9 Ludwigshafen, Ger.....49 27S 8 27 E
28 Luebo, Congo .... 5 21N 21 17 E
14 Lugansk, U.S.S.R. .....48 33N 39 15 E
8 Lugo, Spain...........43 2N 7 35W
12 Luleå, Sweden ....65 35N 22 10 E
28 Luluabourg, Congo.... 5 55S 22 18 E
4 Lundy, I., England 51 10N 4 41W
6 Lurgan, N. Ireland.....54 28N 6 20W
29 Lusaka, Zambia ....15 25S 28 15 E
28 Lusambo, Congo ...... 4 53S 23 14 E
4 Luton, England........51 53N 0 24W
7 Luxembourg, tn. & Duchy, Europe......49 37N 6 9 E
9 Luzern, Switzerland ...47 3N 8 18 E
23 Luzon, I., Philippines ..16 30N 121 30 E
14 Lvov, U.S.S.R. ....49 40N 24 0 E
15 Lyakhov Is., U.S.S.R....73 40N 141 0 E
12 Lycksele, Sweden .....64 38N 18 40 E
7 Lyonnais, Prov., France 45 45N 4 15 E
7 Lyons, France.........45 46N 4 50 E

M

18 Ma'an, Jordan.........30 12N 35 44 E
13 Maarianhamina, Fin. ...60 5N 19 55 E
7 Maastricht, Neth. .....50 50N 5 40 E
20 Macau, China 39 35N 7 59W
4 Macclesfield, England ..53 16N 2 9W
11 Macedonia, Prov., Greece.............41 53N 21 40 E
38 Macdonnell Ra., N. Terr., Australia ..23 40S 133 0 E
37 Maceió, Brazil......... 9 40S 35 41W
6 Macgillycuddy's Reeks, Ireland.............52 2N 9 45W
32 Mackenzie Mts., Can. ..63 0N 131 0W
41 McMurdo Sound, Ant. .77 0S 170 0 E
29 Madagascar, I., (Malagasy Rep.) .....19 0S 46 0 E
24 Madeira, Is., Portugal ..32 50N 17 0W
19 Madhya Pradesh, st., India...............21 50N 81 0 E
35 Madison, U.S.A........43 5N 89 25W
19 Madras, st., India......11 0N 77 0 E
8 Madrid, Spain.........40 25N 3 45W
23 Madura, I., Indon. ..... 7 0S 113 20 E
19 Madurai, India .... 9 55N 78 10 E
21 Maebashi, Japan.......36 30N 139 0 E
28 Mafia, I., Tanzania ..... 7 50S 39 48 E
15 Magadan, U.S.S.R......59 30N 151 0 E
9 Magdeburg, E. Ger.....52 8N 11 36 E
10 Maggiore, L., Italy.....46 0N 8 35 E
14 Magnitogorsk, U.S.S.R..53 20N 59 0 E
19 Maharashtra, st., India .19 30N 76 0 E
29 Mahenge, Tanzania .... 8 45S 36 35 E
4 Maidstone, England....51 16N 0 31 E
27 Maiduguri, Nigeria ....12 0N 13 20 E
9 Main, R., Germany ....50 13N 11 0 E
7 Maine, Prov., France...48 0N 0 0 E
35 Maine, st., U.S.A. 45 20N 69 0W
5 Mainland, Shetland Is., Scotland 60 15N 1 22W
9 Mainz, Germany ......50 0N 8 17 E
8 Majorca, see Mallorca
29 Majunga, Malagasy Rep. 15 40S 46 25 E
23 Makasar, Indonesia .... 5 10S 119 20 E
14 Makeyevka U.S.S.R....48 0N 38 0 E
14 Makhachkala, U.S.S.R. .43 0N 47 15 E
22 Malacca, Malaysia...... 2 15N 102 15 E
8 Malaga, Spain 36 43N 4 23W
29 Malagasy Rep., Africa ..19 0S 46 0 E
27 Malakal, Sudan........ 9 33N 31 50 E
23 Malang, Indonesia ..... 7 59S 112 35 E
29 Malanje, Angola....... 9 30S 16 20 E
29 Malawi, st., Africa .....13 0S 34 0 E
29 Malawi, L., Malawi.....12 0S 34 30 E
22 Malaya, st., Malaysia ... 4 0N 102 0 E
22 Malaysia, Fed. of, Asia.. 5 23N 110 0 E
19 Maldive Is., Indian Oc. . 6 50N 73 0 E
26 Mali, st., W. Africa 17 0N 4 0W
28 Malindi, Kenya........ 3 10S 40 0 E
8 Mallorca (Majorca), I., Spain ....39 30N 3 0 E
6 Mallow, Ireland 52 8N 8 40W

Map
13 Malmo, Sweden ....55 33N 13 8 E
2 Malta, I., Mediterranean Sea................35 50N 14 30 E
23 Manado, Indonesia..... 1 40N 125 45 E
36 Managua, Nicaragua ...12 0N 86 20W
40 Manapouri, L., N.Z. ...45 32S 167 32 E
37 Manaus, Brazil 3 0S 60 0W
8 Mancha, Dist., Spain ...39 5N 2 40W
4 Manchester, England...53 30N 2 15W
29 Manda, Tanzania ......10 30S 34 40 E
13 Mandal, Norway ......58 2N 7 25 E
19 Mandalay, Burma.......22 0N 96 10 E
19 Mangalore, India ......12 55N 74 47 E
37 Manicoré, Brazil....... 6 0S 61 10W
23 Manila, Philippines ....14 40N 121 3 E
32 Manitoba, L., Canada ..50 40N 98 30W
32 Manitoba, Prov., Can...55 30N 97 0W
37 Manizales, Colombia ... 5 10N 75 30W
9 Mannheim, Germany ..49 28N 8 29 E
28 Manono, Congo....... 7 15S 27 20 E
10 Mantua, Italy ....45 9N 10 48 E
37 Maracaibo, Venexuela..10 37N 71 45W
37 Maracay, Venezuela....10 20N 67 35W
7 Marche, Prov., France..46 0N 1 20 E
10 Marches, Reg., Italy....43 22N 13 10 E
36 Margarita I., Venezuela.11 0N 64 0W
4 Margate, England......51 23N 1 24 E
1 Mariana Is., Pacific Oc. .17 0N 145 0 E
36 Marianao, Cuba 23 8N 82 24W
10 Maribor, Y. Slav. ......46 36N 15 40 E
29 Mariental, S W. Africa..24 35S 18 0 E
13 Mariestad, Sweden ....58 42N 13 55 E
1 Marquesas Is., Pacific Ocean 9 30S 140 0W
26 Marrakesh, Morocco...31 40N 8 0W
18 Marsa Fatma, Ethiopia .14 57N 40 17 E
27 Marsa Susa, Libya .....32 52N 21 59 E
10 Marsala, Italy ....37 48N 12 25 E
7 Marseille, France ......43 18N 5 23 E
1 Marshall Is., Pacific Oc.. 9 0N 171 0 E
19 Martaban, Gulf of, Burma ....15 40N 96 30 E
36 Martinique, I., French West Indies 14 40N 61 0W
35 Maryland, st., U.S.A....39 10N 76 40W
21 Masan, S. Korea.......35 15N 128 30 E
36 Masaya, Nicaragua.....12 0N 86 7W
29 Maseru, Lesotho ......29 18S 27 30 E
16 Mashhad, Iran.........36 18N 59 32 E
18 Masqat, Muscat & Oman.............23 38N 58 31 E
10 Massa, Italy ....44 2N 10 7 E
35 Massachusetts, st., U.S.A. 42 25N 72 0W
27 Massakori Chad.......13 0N 15 49 E
7 Massif Central, Mt., France ....45 30N 2 21 E
40 Masterton, N.Z. ......40 56S 175 39 E
19 Masulipatam, India.....16 12N 81 12 E
13 Masurian Lakes, Poland ....53 30N 21 30 E
28 Matadi, Congo .... 5 52S 13 31 E
21 Matsumoto, Japan .....36 15N 138 0 E
21 Matsuyama, Japan .....33 45N 132 45 E
10 Matterhorn, Mt., Switzerland.........45 58N 7 39 E
37 Maturin, Venezuela 9 50N 63 10W
31 Maui, I., Hawaiian Is....21 0N 156 30W
26 Mauritania, st., W. Afr..20 0N 10 0W
1 Mauritius I., Indian Oc..20 0S 57 0 E
36 Mayaguez, Puerto Rico.18 11N 67 8W
6 Mayo, co., Ireland 53 47N 9 7W
16 Mazar-i-Sharif, Afghan..36 0N 67 30 E
28 Mbandaka, Congo ..... 0 1S 18 18 E
34 Mead, L., U.S.A. 36 10N 114 20W
6 Meath, co., Ireland 53 32N 6 40W
18 Mecca, Si. Arabia......21 30N 39 54 E
7 Mechelen, Belg um .....51 2N 4 29 E
22 Medan, Indonesia...... 3 40N 98 38 E
37 Medellin, Colombia.... 6 20N 75 45W
32 Medicine Hat, Canada..50 0N 110 45W
2 Mediterranean Sea, Europe.............35 0N 15 0 E
19 Meerut, India ....29 1N 77 50 E
18 Mekele, Ethiopia ......13 32N 39 28 E
26 Meknès, Morocco 33 57N 5 39W
19 Mekong, R., Asia......18 0N 104 15 E
39 Melbourne, Australia ..37 40S 145 0 E
38 Melville, I., Australia...11 30S 131 0 E
35 Memphis, U.S.A.......35 7N 90 0W
37 Mendoza, Argentina ...32 50S 68 52W
8 Menorca (Minorca), I., Spain ....40 0N 4 0 E
22 Mentawai, Is., Indon.... 2 0S 99 0 E
37 Mercedes, Uruguay....33 12S 58 0W
19 Mergui Arch., Burma ..11 30N 97 30 E
31 Merida, Mexico 20 50N 89 40W
4 Merioneth, co., Wales .52 49N 3 55W
27 Merowe, Sudan ....18 29N 31 46 E
4 Mersey, R., England ...53 20N 2 56W
4 Merthyr-Tydfil, Wales .51 45N 3 23W
28 Meru, Kenya.......... 0 2N 37 35 E
18 Mesewa, Ethiopia......15 35N 39 25 E
18 Mesopotamia, Dist., Iraq ....33 30N 44 0 E
10 Messina, tn. & Str., Sicily, Italy ....38 10N 15 32 E
7 Metz, France..........49 8N 6 10 E
7 Meuse, R., Belgium ....50 32N 5 20 E
30 Mexicali, Mexico 32 40N 115 30W
31 Mexico City, Mexico...19 20N 99 10W
15 0 N to 32 30 N
31 Mexico, Rep., N. America..........87 0W to 117 0W
31 Mexico, Gulf of, America.............25 0N 90 0W
35 Miami, U.S.A..........25 52N 80 15W
20 Miaoli, Taiwan 24 35N 120 53W
35 Michigan, st., U.S A ...44 40N 85 40W
30 Michigan, L , Canada/ U S.A. 44 0N 87 0W
26 Middle Atlas, Mts., Morocco 33 0N 5 0W
4 Middlesbrough, Eng....54 34N 1 13W
5 Midlothian, co., Scot...55 50N 3 15W
1 Midway I., Pacific Oc...28 0N 178 0W
8 Mieres, Spain 43 18N 5 48W
13 Mikkeli, Finland.......61 43N 27 25 E
10 Milan, Italy ....45 28N 9 10 E
4 Milford Haven, Wales..51 43N 5 2W
35 Milwaukee, U.S.A......43 9N 87 58W
23 Mindanao, I., Phil. ..... 8 0N 125 0 E
23 Mindoro, I., Phil.......13 0N 121 0 E
8 Minho, Prov., Portugal.41 43N 8 25W
35 Minneapolis, U.S.A.....44 58N 93 20W
35 Minnesota, st., U.S.A...46 0N 94 30W
14 Minsk, U.S.S.R. ....53 52N 27 30 E
33 Miquelon, I., Canada...47 10N 56 50W

Map
21 Miryang, S. Korea .....35 34N 128 52 E
19 Mirzapur, India ....25 10N 82 45 E
36 Miskito Cays, Nic......14 26S 82 50W
2 Miskolc, Hungary .....48 7N 20 5 E
35 Mississippi, st., U.S.A. .33 0N 90 0W
35 Mississippi, R., U.S.A...41 0N 91 0W
35 Missouri, st., U.S.A. ...38 25N 92 15W
34 Missouri, R., U.S.A. ...38 40N 91 45W
21 Mito, Japan...........36 20N 140 30 E
21 Miyazaki, Japan ....32 0N 131 30 E
35 Mobile, U.S.A.........30 41N 88 3W
10 Módena, Italy.........44 39N 10 55 E
18 Mogadishu, Somali Republic .... 2 2N 45 25 E
14 Moldavia, S.S.R., U.S.S.R.............47 0N 28 0 E
10 Molise, Reg., Italy .....41 45N 14 30 E
31 Molokai, I., Hawaiian Is. 21 10N 157 0W
29 Molopo, R., Africa.....25 40S 24 30 E
15 Molotov, C., U.S.S.R. ..81 10N 95 0 E
28 Mombasa, Kenya ...... 4 0S 39 35 E
7 Monaco, principality, Europe ....43 36N 72 3 E
6 Monaghan, co., Ireland .54 10N 7 0W
20 Mongolia, Rep., Asia...47 0N 103 0 E
29 Mongu, Zambia ....15 16S 23 12 E
4 Monmouth, co., Gt. Brit. 51 43N 3 5W
26 Monrovia, Liberia 6 18N 10 47W
34 Montana, st., U.S.A. ...47 0N 110 0W
36 Montego Bay, Jamaica .18 30N 78 0W
31 Monterrey, Mexico 25 40N 100 30W
37 Montevido, Uruguay...34 50S 56 11W
35 Montgomery, U.S.A....32 20N 86 20W
4 Montgomery, co., Wales 52 37N 3 22W
7 Montpellier, France ...43 37N 3 52 E
33 Montreal, Canada 45 31N 73 34W
7 Montreuil, France 50 27N 1 45W
5 Montrose, Scotland....56 43N 2 28W
36 Montserrat, I., W. I....16 40N 62 10W
32 Moose Jaw, Canada 50 30N 105 30W
19 Moradabad, India......28 50N 78 50 E
9 Moravian Heights, Poland 49 15N 15 0W
9 Moravska Ostrava, Cz..49 50N 18 20 E
5 Moray, co., Scotland ...57 32N 3 25W
5 Moray Firth, Scot......57 50N 3 30W
4 Morecambe, England ..54 5N 2 52W
21 Morioka, Japan ....39 45N 141 8 E
26 Morocco, st., N. Afr. ..32 0N 5 0W
29 Morondava, Malagasy Republic ....20 25S 44 30 E
14 Moscow (Moskva), U.S.S.R.............55 45N 37 35 E
9 Moselle, R., Germany..49 48N 6 45 E
28 Moshi, Tanzania....... 3 18S 37 27 E
12 Mosjöen, Norway .....65 52N 13 20 E
29 Mossamedes, Angola...15 7S 12 11 E
29 Mossel Bay, S. Africa ..34 11S 22 8 E
5 Motherwell, Scotland ..55 48N 4 0W
19 Moulmein, Burma .....16 30N 97 40 E
38 Mount Goldsworthy, Australia...........20 25S 119 35 E
39 Mount Isa, Australia ...20 42S 139 26 E
38 Mount Newman, Australia...........23 23S 119 25 E
38 Mount Nicholas, Australia...........22 40S 120 20 E
7 Mount St. Michel, Fr. ..48 40N 1 35W
38 Mount Tom Price, Australia...........22 47S 117 40 E
31 Mountain View, Alas. ..61 7N 149 53W
6 Mourne Mts., N. Ire. ..54 10N 6 0W
29 Mozambique, Port. Col. Afr.......23 30S 32 30 E
22 Muar, Malaysia........ 2 3N 102 34 E
29 Mufulira Zambia......12 30S 28 0 E
18 Mukalla, S. Yemen ....14 33N 49 2 E
20 Mukden, China ....41 50N 123 30 E
9 Mulheim, Germany ....51 26N 6 53 E
7 Mulhouse, France .....47 44N 7 20 E
5 Mull I., Scotland 56 27N 6 0W
19 Multan, W. Pakistan ...30 15N 71 30 E
9 München Gladbach, Germany...........51 12N 6 23 E
9 Munich (München) Germany...........48 8N 11 35 E
9 Münster, Germany ....51 58N 7 37 E
6 Munster, Prov., Ireland 52 20N 8 40 E
8 Murcia, Spain 38 2N 1 10W
8 Murcia, Prov., Spain ...38 35N 1 50W
14 Murmansk, U.S.S.R. ...68 57N 33 10 E
21 Muroran, Japan ....42 25N 141 0 E
39 Murray, R., Austral. ...35 50S 147 40 E
39 Murray Bridge, Austral.35 6S 139 14 E
18 Muscat and Oman, Sultanate, Asia......23 0N 58 0 E
5 Musselburgh, Scot. 55 57N 3 3W
20 Mutankiang, China ....43 50N 129 30 E
28 Mwanza, Tanzania ..... 2 30S 33 0 E
19 Myitkyina, Burma .....25 30S 97 26 E
19 Mysore, India ....12 17N 76 41 E
19 Mysore, st., India......13 15N 77 0 E

N

17 Nablus, Jordan........32 14N 35 15 E
13 Næstved, Denmark....55 13N 11 44 E
19 Naga Hills, India/Burma ....27 0N 95 30 E
21 Nagano, Japan ....36 40N 138 10 E
21 Nagaoka, Japan ....37 30N 138 50 E
19 Nagapattinam, India ...10 46N 79 51 E
21 Nagasaki, Japan ....32 47N 129 50 E
19 Nagercoil, India........ 8 12N 77 33 E
21 Nagoya, Japan ....35 10N 136 50 E
19 Nagpur, India.........21 8N 79 10 E
5 Nairn, co., Scotland ...57 35N 3 54W
28 Nairobi, Kenya .... 1 20S 36 50 E
28 Nakuru, Kenya .... 0 15S 36 5 E
22 Nam Dinh, N. Viet. ...20 25N 106 5 E
14 Namangan, U.S.S.R. ...41 30N 71 30 E
12 Namsos, Norway......64 28N 11 35 E
20 Nanchang, China......28 40N 115 45 E
7 Nancy, France ....48 42N 6 12 E
20 Nanking, China ....32 10N 118 50 E
20 Nanning, China ....22 52N 108 5 E
7 Nantes, France........47 12N 1 33W
40 Napier, N.Z. ....39 30S 176 56 E
10 Naples (Napoli), Italy ..40 40N 14 5 E
17 Naqura, Lebanon......33 7N 35 8 E
21 Nara, Japan ....34 40N 135 59 E
7 Narbonne, France .....43 11N 3 0 E
12 Narvik, Norway ......68 28N 17 35 E
35 Nashville, U.S.A.......36 12N 86 46 E
36 Nassau, Bahamas 25 0N 77 30W

Map
37 Natal, Brazil 5 50S 35 10W
29 Natal, Prov., S. Afr. ...28 30S 30 30 E
1 Nauru I., Pacific Ocean 9 25S 166 0 E
6 Navan, Ireland 53 39N 6 40W
8 Navarra, Prov., Spain ..42 40N 1 40W
11 Náxos, I., Greece .....37 5N 25 30 E
17 Nazareth, Israel ....32 42N 35 17 E
28 N'Djole, Gabon .... 0 5S 10 45 E
6 Neagh, L., N. Ireland ..54 35N 6 25W
31 Near Is., Aleutian Is....53 0N 172 0 E
34 Nebraska, st., U.S.A. ..41 30N 100 0W
23 Negros, I., Philippines .10 0N 123 0 E
20 Neikiang, China.......29 35N 105 10 E
40 Nelson, N.Z. ....41 18S 173 16 E
19 Nepal, King., Asia.....28 0N 84 30 E
12 Neskaupstadur, Iceland 65 10N 13 43W
5 Ness, L., Scotland 57 15N 4 30W
17 Netanya, Israel........32 20N 34 51 E
7 Netherlands, King., Europe ....52 0N 5 30 E
9 Neuchâtel, Switzerland 46 53N 6 50 E
9 Neuchâtel, L., Switz. ..46 53N 6 50 E
9 Neumünster, Germany 54 4N 9 58 E
34 Nevada, st., U.S.A.....39 0N 117 0W
7 Nevers, France ....47 0N 3 9 E
37 New Amsterdam, Guyana 6 15N 57 30W
35 New Bedford, U.S.A. ..41 40N 70 52W
33 New Brunswick, Prov., Canada 46 50N 66 30W
1 New Caledonia Arch., Pacific Ocean ....21 0S 165 0 E
8 New Castile, Prov., Spain 39 45N 3 20W
1 New Guinea, I., Australasia .... 4 0S 136 0 E
35 New Hampshire, st., U.S.A. 43 40N 71 40W
35 New Haven, U.S.A. ...41 20N 72 54W
1 New Hebrides Is., Pacific Ocean ....15 0S 168 0 E
35 New Jersey, st., U.S.A. 39 50N 74 10W
34 New Mexico, st., U.S.A. 34 30N 106 0W
35 New Orleans, U.S.A. ..30 0N 90 0W
40 New Plymouth, N.Z. ..39 4S 174 5 E
36 New Providence I., Bahamas 25 0N 77 30W
4 New Quay, Wales.....52 13N 4 21W
15 New Siberian Is., U.S.S.R.............65 0N 140 0 E
39 New South Wales, st., Australia...........33 0S 146 0 E
32 New Westminster, Canada 49 10N 122 52W
35 New York, U.S.A......40 45N 74 0W
35 New York, st., U.S.A. .42 40N 76 0W
40 New Zealand, st., Br. Commonwealth .41 0S 175 0 E
4 Newark, England......53 6N 0 48W
35 Newark, U.S.A........40 41N 74 12W
4 Newbury, England 51 24N 1 19W
39 Newcastle, Australia...32 52S 5 49 E
4 Newcastle, England....54 58N 1 37W
4 Newcastle under Lyme, England 53 2N 2 15W
33 Newfoundland, Prov., Canada 48 28N 56 0W
4 Newport, Wales 52 1N 4 51W
35 Newport News, U.S.A. 37 0N 76 25W
4 Newquay, England 50 24N 5 6W
6 Newry, N. Ireland 54 10N 6 20W
6 Newtownards, N. Ire. .54 37N 5 40W
28 Ngaoundéré, Cam. .... 7 15N 13 35 E
35 Niagara Falls, U.S.A....43 5N 79 5W
28 Niangara, Congo ...... 8 47N 27 59 E
22 Nias, I., Indonesia ..... 1 0N 97 40 E
36 Nicaragua, st., Central America 11 40N 85 30W
36 Nicaragua, La., Central America 12 50N 85 30W
7 Nice, France..........43 42N 7 14 E
19 Nicobar Is., India...... 9 0N 93 0 E
2 Nicosia, Cyprus.......35 10N 33 25 E
26 Niger, st., Africa ......15 30N 10 0 E
26 Niger, R., W. Africa...13 35N 7 0 E
26 Nigeria, st., W. Africa . 8 30N 8 0 E
21 Niigata, Japan ....37 58N 139 0 E
31 Niihau, I., Hawaii 21 50N 160 11W
7 Nijmegen, Neth. ......51 50N 5 52 E
14 Nikolayev, U.S.S.R.....46 58N 32 7 E
15 Nikolayevsk, U.S.S.R...53 30N 140 50 E
27 Nile, R., Egypt........27 30N 30 30 E
7 Nîmes, France ....43 50N 4 23 E
20 Ningpo, China ....29 50N 121 30 E
20 Ningsia Hui, Autonomous Region, China...............37 15N 106 0 E
11 Nis, Yugoslavia ....43 19N 21 58 E
37 Niteroi, Brazil 22 52S 43 0W
7 Nivernais, Prov., France ....47 0N 3 40 E
15 Nizhneudinsk, U.S.S.R. 55 0N 99 20 E
14 Nizhniy Tagil, U.S.S.R..57 45N 60 0 E
21 Nogata, Japan ....33 48N 130 54 E
31 Nome, Alaska 64 35N 165 40W
15 Nordvik, U.S.S.R. .....73 40N 110 57 E
35 Norfolk, U.S.A........42 3N 97 25W
4 Norfolk, co., England ..52 39N 1 0 E
1 Norfolk I., Pacific Oc...28 58S 168 3 E
7 Normandie, Prov., France 49 0N 0 0
13 Norrköping, Sweden ..58 35N 16 10 E
1 North America, cont... 10 to 80 N 20 to 120W
33 North Bay, Canada 46 20N 79 30W
35 North Carolina, st., U.S.A. 35 30N 79 0W
34 North Dakota, st., U.S.A. 47 0N 100 0W
40 North Island, N.Z. ....38 0S 175 0 E
21 North Korea, st., Asia ....40 0N 127 0 E
41 North Pole, Arctic.....90 0N
9 North Rhine, –Westphalia, land, Germany...........52 0N 8 0 E
2 North Sea, Europe ....55 0N 4 9 E
11 North Sporades, Is., Greece ....39 0N 24 10 E
5 North Uist I., Scot.....57 40N 7 15W
22 North Vietnam, st., Asia ....22 0N 105 0 E
32 Northwest Territories, Canada 65 0N 100 0W
4 Northampton, England 52 14N 0 54W
4 Northampton, co., England 52 16N 0 55W

Map
6 Northern Ireland, United Kingdom 54 45N 7 0W
38 Northern Territory, Australia...........16 0S 133 0 E
4 Northumberland, co., England 55 12N 2 0W
31 Norton Sound, Alaska .63 50N 164 0W
12 Norway, King, Eur. ...67 0N 11 0 E
4 Norwich, England .....52 38N 1 17 E
4 Nottingham, England ..52 57N 1 10W
4 Nottingham, co., Eng. .53 10N 1 0W
26 Nouakchott, Mauritania18 20N 15 50W
29 Nova Lisboa, Angola...12 42S 15 54W
33 Nova Scotia, Prov., Canada 45 10N 63 0W
10 Novara, Italy ....45 27N 8 36 E
41 Novaya Zemlya Is., U.S.S.R.............75 0N 56 0 E
11 Novi Sad, Y.-Slav. .....45 18N 19 52 E
14 Novokuznetsk, U.S.S.R.55 0N 83 5 E
14 Novorossiysk, U.S.S.R..44 43N 37 52 E
14 Novosibirsk, U.S.S.R...55 0N 83 5 E
21 Numazu, Japan ....35 15N 139 5 E
4 Nuneaton, England 52 32N 1 29W
9 Nurnberg (Nuremberg), Germany...........49 26N 11 5 E
27 Nyala, Sudan ....12 2N 24 58 E
13 Nybro, Sweden ....55 20N 10 49 E
13 Nyköbing, Denmark...54 46N 11 52 E

O

31 Oahu, I., Hawaiian Is. ..21 30N 158 0W
4 Oakham, England 52 40N 0 43W
40 Oamaru, N.Z. ....45 5S 170 59 E
14 Ob, R., U.S.S.R........62 40N 66 0 E
5 Oban, Scotland 56 25N 5 30W
18 Obbia, Somali Rep..... 5 25N 48 30 E
9 Oberhausen, Ger......51 30N 6 50W
37 Obidos, Brazil 1 50S 55 30W
21 Odawara, Japan ....35 20N 139 6 E
13 Odense, Denmark.....55 26N 10 26 E
14 Odessa, U.S.S.R. ......41 30S 30 45 E
9 Odra (Oder) R., Pol. ..53 0N 14 12 E
6 Offaly, co., Ireland 53 15N 7 30W
9 Offenbach, Germany...50 6N 8 46 E
26 Ogbomosho, Nigeria .. 8 1N 3 29 E
34 Ogden, U.S.A. 41 13N 112 1W
35 Ohio st., U.S.A. 40 20N 83 0W
35 Ohio, R., U.S.A. 39 50N 80 50W
21 Oita, Japan ....33 15N 131 36 E
29 Okavango Swamp Botswana ....19 30S 23 0 E
21 Okayama, Japan.......34 40N 133 44 E
15 Okhotsk, U.S.S.R......59 20N 143 10 E
15 Okhotsk, Sea of, U.S.S.R.............55 0N 154 0 E
21 Oki, I., Japan ....36 15N 133 15 E
29 Okiep, S. Africa.......29 39S 17 53 E
20 Okinawa, I., Ryukyu Is. 27 10N 128 0 E
34 Oklahoma, st., U.S.A...35 40N 97 0W
34 Oklahoma City, U.S.A. 35 25N 97 30W
21 Okushiri, I., Japan ....42 15N 139 30 E
13 Öland, I., Sweden .....56 45N 16 50 E
37 Olavarria, Argentina...36 55S 60 20W
8 Old Castile, Prov., Sp. .41 55N 4 0W
9 Oldenburg, Germany ..53 10N 8 10 E
4 Oldham, England 53 33N 2 8W
15 Olekminsk, U.S.S.R....60 40N 120 30 E
29 Olifants, R., S. Africa ..24 5S 31 20 E
11 Olympia, site, Greece..37 39N 21 39 E
11 Olympus, Mt., Greece .40 6N 22 23 E
6 Omagh, N. Ireland 54 36N 7 20W
35 Omaha, U.S.A.........41 15N 96 0W
18 Oman, Gulf of, S. W. Asia ....24 30N 58 30 E
27 Omdurman, Sudan ....15 40N 32 28 E
21 Omiya, Japan ....36 0N 139 32 E
14 Omsk, U.S.S.R. ....55 0N 73 38 E
21 Omuta, Japan.........33 0N 130 26 E
14 Onega, U.S.S.R........64 0N 38 10 E
40 Onehunga, N.Z. ......36 55N 174 50 E
38 Onslow, Australia .....21 40S 115 0 E
21 Ontake Mt., Japan ....35 50N 137 15 E
33 Ontario, Prov., Can....52 0N 88 10W
30 Ontario, L., Canada/U.S.A. 43 40N 78 0W
7 Oostende, Belgium ....51 14N 2 55 E
9 Opava, Cz. ....49 57N 17 58 E
8 Oporto, Portugal 41 8N 8 40W
11 Oradea, Rumania......47 2N 21 58 E
26 Oran, Algeria.........36 45N 0 39W
29 Orange, R., S. Africa ..29 50S 24 45 E
29 Orange Free State, Prov., S. Africa .....28 30S 27 0 E
14 Ordzhonikidze, U.S.S.R.43 0N 44 30 E
13 Orebro, Sweden ......59 20N 15 18 E
34 Oregon, st., U.S.A.....44 0N 120 0W
14 Orel, U.S.S.R. ....52 57N 36 3 E
14 Orenburg, U.S.S.R.....52 0N 55 5 E
8 Orense, Spain 42 19N 7 55W
37 Orinoco, R., Ven. 8 0N 65 30W
19 Orissa, st., India ......21 0N 85 0 E
5 Orkney, co., Scot......59 0N 3 0W
5 Orkney Is., Scotland ...59 0N 3 0W
7 Orleanais, Prov., Fr. ...47 55N 1 0 E
7 Orléans, France ....47 54N 1 52 E
23 Ormoc, Philippines ....11 2N 124 30 E
13 Örnsköldsvik, Sweden .63 17N 18 50 E
37 Oruro, Bolivia 18 0S 67 19W
21 Osaka, Japan ....34 40N 135 30 E
33 Oshawa, Canada 43 50N 78 45W
26 Oshogbo, Nigeria ..... 7 48N 4 37 E
11 Osijek, Yugoslavia.....43 34N 18 41 E
13 Oskarshamn, Sweden ..57 15N 16 25 E
13 Oslo, Norway ....59 53N 10 52 E
9 Osnabruck, Germany ..52 16N 8 2 E
37 Osorno, Chile 40 25S 73 0W
13 Östersund, Sweden....63 10N 14 45 E
21 Osumi Group, Is., Japan ....30 30N 130 45 E
4 Oswestry, England 52 52N 3 3W
21 Otaru, Japan ....43 15N 141 0 E
29 Otavi, S. W. Africa....19 40S 17 24 E
11 Otranto, Str. of, Adriatic Sea ....40 15N 18 40 E
21 Otsu, Japan ....42 35N 143 40 E
33 Ottawa, Canada.......45 27N 75 42W
28 Ouadda, Cent. Africa .. 8 15N 22 20 E
28 Ouanda Djale, Central Africa ...... 8 55N 22 53 E
28 Ouesso, Congo .... 1 40N 16 10 E
26 Oujda, Morocco.......34 45N 2 0W
12 Oulu, Finland ....64 58N 25 40 E
12 Oulu, R., Finland .....64 25N 27 30 E
5 Outer Hebrides, Is., Scotland 57 30N 7 40W
8 Oviedo, Spain 43 25N 5 50W
4 Oxford & co., England .51 45N 1 15W

(x) 9/70

Map

P

22 Padang, Indonesia .... 1 0S 100 20 E
10 Padua, Italy .... .45 24N 11 52 E
10 Pag, I., Yugoslavia ....44 50N 15 0 E
23 Pagadian, I., Phil. .. 7 55N 123 30 E
3 Paisley, Scotland 55 51N 4 27W
19 Pakistan, East ...... 24 0N 90 0 E
19 Pakistan, West....... .30 0N 70 0 E
22 Palembang, Indonesia .. 3 0S 104 50 E
8 Palencia, Spain 42 1N 4 34W
10 Palermo, Sicily, Italy..38 8N 13 20 E
8 Palma, Mallorca, Sp. ..39 33N 2 39 E
40 Palmerston North,
     New Zealand ......40 21S 175 39 E
8 Pamplona, Spain 42 48N 1 38W
36 Panama, Rep.,
     S. America 9 0N 79 35W
36 Panama, tn. & canal,
     Central America ... 9 0N 79 25W
23 Panay, I. Philippines ..11 0N 122 30 E
19 Panjim, Goa, India....15 25N 73 50 E
10 Pantelleria, I., Italy ...36 52N 12 0 E
20 Paoki, China.........34 25N 107 15 E
20 Paoting, China.......38 50N 115 30 E
20 Paotow, China.......40 45N 110 0 E
40 Papakura, N.Z. ....37 4S 174 59 E
1 Papua, Terr. of,
     New Guinea ...... 8 0S 145 0 E
37 Pará, R., Brazil....... 0 40S 48 30W
37 Paraguay, Rep.,
     S. America ....21 0S to 27 30S
                   54 15W to 61 20W
37 Paramaribo, Surinam . 5 50N 55 10W
37 Parana, Argentina 32 0S 60 30W
21 Pardubice, Cz........50 3N 15 45 E
7 Paris, France........48 50N 2 20 E
21 Parma, Italy ....44 50N 10 20 E
34 Pasadena, U.S.A. 34 5N 118 0W
19 Patna, India.........25 35N 85 18 E
11 Patrai, Greece ....38 14N 21 47 E
7 Pau, France 43 19N 0 25W
37 Paysandú, Uruguay ...32 19S 58 8W
17 Pearl Harbor, Hawaii ..21 20N 158 0W
9 Péces, Hungary ....46 5N 18 15 E
5 Peebles, co., Scot. 55 40N 3 12W
19 Pegu. Burma........17 20N 96 29 E
20 Pehpei, China........29 50N 106 23 E
22 Pekalongan, Indonesia.. 6 53S 109 40 N
20 Peking, China........39 50N 116 20 E
11 Peloponnese, Prov.,
     Greece ....37 10N 22 0 E
37 Pelotas, Brazil 31 42S 52 23W
28 Pemba, I., Tanzania .. 5 20S 39 40 E
4 Pembroke, co., Wales .51 40N 5 0W
22 Penang, I., Malaysia .. 5 25N 100 15 E
20 Pengpu, China........33 0N 117 25 E
20 Penki, China.........41 20N 123 50 E
35 Pennsylvania, st.,
     U.S.A. 40 50N 78 0W
4 Penrith, England 54 40N 2 45W
14 Penza, U.S.S.R. ......53 15N 45 5 E
4 Penzance, England 50 7N 5 32W
35 Peoria, U.S.A. 40 40N 89 40W
37 Pereira, Colombia 4 50N 75 40W
7 Périgueux, France ....45 10N 0 42 E
18 Perim, I., Gulf of Aden.12 38N 43 25 E
14 Perm, U.S.S.R. ....58 0N 56 10 E
7 Perpignan, France ....42 42N 2 53 E
18 Persian Gulf, Asia ....27 0N 50 0 E
38 Perth, Australia ......31 57S 115 52 E
5 Perth, Scotland 56 24N 3 27W
5 Perth, co., Scot. 56 30N 4 0W
37 Peru, Rep., S. Amer. . 2 30 S to 18 0 S
                   69 0W to 81 15W
10 Perugia, Italy ....43 6N 12 24 E
10 Pescara, Italy ....42 28N 14 13 E
19 Peshawar, W. Pakistan.34 2N 71 37 E
17 Petah Tiqwa, Israel ...32 6N 34 53 E
4 Peterborough, Eng....52 35N 0 14W
5 Peterhead, Scotland ...57 30N 1 49W
40 Petone, N.Z. ....41 13S 174 53 E
14 Petropavlovsk, U.S.S.R. 55 0N 69 0 E
37 Petropolis, Brazil.....22 33S 43 9W
14 Petrozavodsk, U.S.S.R..61 41N 34 20 E
9 Pforzheim, Germany...48 53N 8 43 E
5 Phan Rang, S. Vietnam.11 40N 109 9 E
22 Phanom Dong Rahek,
     Mts., Thailand .....14 40N 104 0 E
35 Philadelphia, U.S.A. ..40 0N 75 10W
23 Philippines Is., Rep.,
     Asia ....12 0N 123 0 E
22 Phnom Penh,
     Cambodia ....11 33N 104 55 E
34 Phoenix, U.S.A. 33 30N 112 10W
10 Piacenza, Italy ....45 3N 9 41 E
7 Picardie, Prov., Fr. ...50 0N 2 15 E
10 Piedmont, Reg., Italy ..45 0N 7 50 E
13 Pietarsaari, Finland ..63 41N 22 40 E
9 Pietermaritzburg,
     S. Africa ....29 35S 30 25 E
29 Pietersburg, S. Africa .23 54S 29 25 E
11 Pindus, Mts., Greece ..40 0N 21 0 E
20 Pingtung, Taiwan .....22 40N 120 30 E
36 Pinos, I. de, Cuba 21 40N 82 40W
11 Piraievs, Greece......37 57N 23 42 E
10 Pisa, Italy ....43 43N 10 23 E
10 Pistóia, Italy ....43 57N 10 53 E
1 Pitcairn I., Pacific Oc. . 5 S 130 5W
12 Pitea, Sweden ....65 55N 21 25 E
35 Pittsburgh, U.S.A. 40 25N 79 55W
37 Piura, Peru 5 5S 80 45W
9 Plauen, E. Germany ...50 29N 12 9 E
9 Pleven, Bulgaria .....43 26N 24 37 E
11 Ploești, Rumania .....44 57N 26 5 E
11 Plovdiv, Bulgaria .....42 8N 24 44 E
4 Plymouth, England ...50 23N 4 9W
21 Plzen, Cz. ....49 45N 13 22 E
21 Pohang, S. Korea.....36 3N 129 26 E
28 Pointe Noire, Congo
     (Fr.) .... 4 48S 12 0 E
7 Poitiers, France 46 35N 0 20W
7 Poitou, Prov., France .46 30N 0 1W
2 Poland, st., Europe ...52 0N 20 0 E
14 Poltava, U.S.S.R. .....49 35N 34 35 E
36 Ponce, P. Rico 18 0N 66 50W
19 Pondicherry, India....11 59N 79 50 E
37 Ponta Grossa, Brazil..25 0S 50 10W
8 Pontevedra, Spain 42 26N 8 40W
22 Pontianak, Indonesia .. 0 3S 109 15 E
4 Pontypool, Wales 51 42N 3 1W
4 Poole, England 50 42N 2 2W
19 Poona, India.........18 29N 73 57 E
13 Pori, Finland ....61 27N 21 50 E
33 Port Arthur, Canada . .48 20N 89 10W
36 Port au Prince, Haiti ..18 40N 72 20W
29 Port Elizabeth,
     S. Africa ....33 58S 25 40 E

4 Port Erin, I. of Man,
     Great Britain 54 5N 4 45W
26 Port Etienne,
     Mauritania 21 0N 17 0W
28 Port Gentil, Gabon ... 0 47S 8 40 E
5 Port Glasgow, Scot. ...55 57N 4 40W
26 Port Harcourt, Nigeria 4 40N 7 10 E
38 Port Hedland,
     Australia ....20 25S 118 35 E
6 Port Laoise, Ireland ...53 2N 7 20W
1 Port Moresby, Papua . 9 24S 147 8 E
29 Port Nolloth, S. Afr. ..29 17S 16 52 E
36 Port of Spain, Trin. ...10 40N 61 20W
27 Port Said, Egypt .....31 16N 32 18 E
27 Port Sudan, Sudan ...19 32N 37 9 E
6 Portadown, N. Ireland .54 27N 6 26W
32 Portage la Prairie,
     Canada 49 58N 98 18W
35 Portland, Maine,
     U.S.A. 43 40N 70 15W
34 Portland, Oregon,
     U.S.A. 45 35N 122 40W
37 Pôrto Alegre, Brazil ..30 5S 51 3W
29 Porto Amelia, Mozam..30 0S 40 42 E
26 Porto Novo, Dahomey. 6 28N 2 42 E
4 Portsmouth, England .50 48N 1 6W
35 Portsmouth, U.S.A. ...36 50N 76 20W
8 Portugal, Rep., Eur. ..40 0N 7 0W
26 Portuguese Guinea,
     W. Africa 12 0N 15 0W
37 Potosi, Bolivia 19 38S 65 50W
13 Potsdam, E. Ger. .....52 23N 13 4 E
9 Poznan, Poland ......52 25N 17 0 E
21 Prague, Cz. ....50 5N 14 22 E
4 Preston, England 53 46N 2 42W
5 Prestwick, Scotland ...55 30N 4 38W
29 Pretoria, S. Africa ....25 44S 28 12 E
32 Prince Albert, Canada .53 15N 105 50W
33 Prince Edward I.,
     Canada 46 15N 63 0W
1 Prince Edward Is.,
     Rep., of S. Africa ...46 25S 37 30 E
32 Prince George, Can. ..53 50N 122 50W
31 Prince of Wales I.,
     Alaska 55 30N 132 30W
39 Prince of Wales I.,
     Australia ....10 35S 142 0 E
32 Prince of Wales, I.,
     Canada 73 0N 99 0W
41 Prince Patrick I.,
     Canada 77 0N 120 0W
32 Prince Rupert, Can. ..54 20N 130 20W
14 Prokopyevsk, U.S.S.R..54 0N 87 3 E
19 Prome, Burma ......18 45N 95 30 E
7 Provence, Prov., Fr. ..43 40N 4 46 E
35 Providence, U.S.A. ...41 41N 71 15W
36 Providencia, I.,
     Caribbean Sea 13 25N 81 26W
11 Prut, R., Rumania ...46 3N 28 10 E
14 Pskov, U.S.S.R. ......57 50N 28 25 E
36 Puebla, Mexico 19 0N 98 10W
34 Pueblo, U.S.A. 38 20N 104 40W
36 Puerto Rico, I.,
     W. Indies 18 10N 66 30W
10 Pula, Yugoslavia .....44 54N 13 57 E
19 Punjab,st., India......31 0N 75 0 E
36 Puntarenas, Costa Rica.10 0N 84 50W
21 Pusan, S. Korea......35 5N 129 0 E
21 Pyongyang, N. Korea .39 0N 125 30 E
7 Pyrenees, Mts.,
     France–Spain .....42 45N 1 0 E

Q

17 Qalqiliya, Jordan .....32 12N 34 58 m
18 Qatar, st., Asia ....25 30N 51 15 E
17 Qeshm, I., Iran ......26 50N 55 45 E
17 Qir Yam, Israel ......32 28N 35 7 E
18 Qizan, Saudi Arabia ..16 57N 42 34 E
33 Quebec, Canada 46 52N 71 13W
33 Quebec, Prov.,
     Canada ....45 0 N to 62 30 N
                   57 0W to 80 0W
32 Queen Charlotte, Is.,
     Canada 53 10N 132 0W
41 Queen Maud Land,
     Antarctica ....75 0S 10 0 E
39 Queensland, st.,
     Australia ....10 40 S to 29 0 S
                   138 0 E to 153 30 E
29 Quelimane, Mozam....17 53S 36 58 E
19 Quetta, W. Pakistan ..30 16N 66 55 E
23 Quezon City, Phil. ....14 50N 121 0 E
37 Quito, Ecuador 0 15S 78 35W

R

26 Rabat, Morocco 33 9N 6 53W
4 Radnor, co., Wales ...52 20N 3 20W
10 Ragusa, Sicily, Italy ..36 56N 14 42 E
19 Rajasthan, st., India...26 45N 73 30 E
19 Rajkot, India.........22 15N 70 56 E
17 Ramallah, Jordan ....31 55N 35 10 E
17 Ramat Gan, Israel ....32 4N 34 48 E
19 Rampur, India.......28 50N 79 5 E
13 Randers, Denmark ...56 29N 10 1 E
19 Rangoon, Burma .....16 45N 96 20 E
19 Rangpur, E. Pakistan..24 42N 89 22 E
1 Rapa Nui I., Pacific Oc.27 0S 109 0W
18 Rasht, Iran ....37 20N 49 40 E
31 Rat Is., Aleutian Is. ...51 48N 178 5 E
6 Rathlin, I., N. Ireland .55 18N 6 14W
13 Rauma, Finland ....61 10N 21 30 E
13 Ravenna, Italy ....44 28N 12 15 E
19 Rawalpindi, W. Pak...33 38N 73 8 E
4 Reading, England 51 27N 0 57W
21 Rebun, I., Japan .....45 28N 141 0 E
37 Recife, Brazil 8 0S 35 0W
18 Red Sea, Afr./Si. Arab..25 0N 36 0 E
9 Regensburg, Germany .49 1N 12 7 E
10 Reggio, Italy ....38 7N 15 38 E
32 Regina, Canada 50 30N 104 35W
17 Rehovot, Israel ......31 54N 34 48 E
4 Reigate, England 51 14N 0 11W
7 Reims, France ....49 15N 4 0 E
9 Remscheid, Germany ..51 11N 7 12 E
5 Renfrew, co., Scot. ...55 50N 4 34W
7 Rennes, France 48 7N 1 41W
34 Reno, U.S.A. 39 30N 119 50W
37 Resistencia, Argentina .27 30N 59 0W
1 Réunion I., Indian Oc...22 0S 56 0 E
37 Revilla Gigedo Is.,
     Pacific Oc.........18 40N 112 0W
12 Reykjavik, Iceland 64 10N 22 0W
9 Rhine, R., Germany ...51 0N 7 0 E
9 Rhine-Land, Palatinate,
     Land, Germany ....50 0N 7 0 E
29 Rhodesia, st., Africa ..19 0S 29 0 E
11 Rhodope Mts., Bulgaria 41 40N 24 20 E
4 Rhondda, Wales 51 40N 3 30W

7 Rhône, R., France .....43 28N 4 42 E
4 Rhyl, Wales 53 19N 3 29W
8 Ribatejo, Prov., Port. ..39 10N 8 30 E
37 Ribeirão Preto,
     Brazil 21 10S 47 50W
35 Richmond, U.S.A. 37 33N 77 27W
9 Riesen G. (Giant Mts.),
     Poland ....50 50N 16 0 E
13 Riga, U.S.S.R. ....56 58N 24 12 E
13 Riga, Gulf of, U.S.S.R..57 40N 23 45 E
10 Rijeka, Yugoslavia ....45 20N 14 21 E
10 Rimini, Italy ....44 3N 12 33 E
37 Rio Cuarto, Argentina .33 10S 64 25W
37 Rio de Janeiro, Brazil..22 50S 43 0W
37 Rio Gallegos, Arg.....51 45S 69 20W
34 Rio Grande, R., U.S.A..35 45N 106 20W
28 Rio Muni,Sp. Col.,
     W. Africa .... 1 30N 10 0 E
37 Riobamba, Ecuador ... 1 50S 78 45W
37 Rivera, Uruguay 31 0S 55 50W
10 Riviera di Levante,
     Italy ....44 23N 9 15 E
33 Rivière du Loup, Can. .47 50N 69 30W
26 Robertsport, Liberia .. 6 45N 11 26 E
37 Rocha, Uruguay 34 30S 54 25W
7 Rochefort, France 45 56N 0 57W
35 Rochester, U.S.A. 43 10N 77 40W
35 Rockford, U.S.A. 42 20N 89 0W
30 Rocky Mts., N. Amer. .48 0N 113 0W
11 Rodhos (Rhodes) I.,
     Greece ....36 15N 28 10 E
10 Rome, Italy ....41 54N 12 30 E
37 Rosario, Argentina ...33 0S 60 50W
6 Roscommon, co., Ire ..53 49N 8 20W
36 Roseau, Dominica 15 20N 61 30W
13 Roskilde, Denmark ...55 38N 12 3 E
41 Ross & Cromarty, co.,
     Scotland 57 43N 4 50W
41 Ross Dependency,
     Antarctica 70 0S 170 5W
13 Rostock, Germany ....54 4N 12 9 E
14 Rostov, U.S.S.R. .....47 15N 39 45 E
4 Rotherham, England ..53 26N 1 21W
40 Rotorua, N.Z. ....38 9S 176 16 E
7 Rotterdam, Neth. .....51 55N 4 30 E
7 Roubaix, France .....50 40N 3 10 E
7 Rouen, France ....49 27N 1 4 E
33 Rouyn, Canada 48 20N 79 0W
5 Roxburgh & co.,
     Scotland 55 34N 2 30W
18 Rub al Khali, Desert,
     Saudi Arabia ......21 0N 51 0 E
28 Rudolf, L., Kenya .... 3 40N 30 20 E
9 Rugby, England 52 23N 1 16W
9 Rügen, I., E. Germany .54 22N 13 25 E
19 Rum Jungle, Australia .13 20S 131 4 E
11 Rumania, st., Europe ..46 0N 25 0 E
11 Ruse, Bulgaria ....43 48N 25 59 E
14 Russian Soviet Federal
     Socialist Rep.,
     U.S.S.R..........43 0 N to 80 0 N
                   28 0 E to 180 0 E
4 Rutland, co., England .52 38N 0 40W
28 Rwanda, st., Africa .. 2 30S 30 0 E
14 Ryazan, U.S.S.R. .....54 0N 39 40 E
21 Ryukyu, Is., Asia .....26 0N 127 0 E

S

9 Saar, Land, Germany .49 20N 0 75 E
9 Saarbrucken, Germany.49 15N 6 58 E
8 Sabadell, Spain ......41 28N 2 7 E
23 Sabah (N. Borneo)
     Malaysia .... 6 0 E 117 0 E
34 Sacramento, U.S.A. ..38 39N 121 30 E
21 Sado, I., Japan ....38 15N 138 30 E
26 Safi, Morocco 32 25N 9 9W
26 Sagaing, Burma ......22 0N 96 0 E
26 Sahara Desert, Afr....23 0N 5 0W
26 Saharan Atlas Mts.,
     Algeria ....34 9N 3 29 E
19 Saharanpur, India ....30 58N 77 33 E
22 Saigon–Cholon, S. Viet.10 58N 106 40 E
4 St. Albans, England ...51 44N 0 19W
5 St. Andrews, Scotland .56 20N 2 48W
5 St. Austell, England ...50 20N 4 48W
32 St. Boniface, Canada ..49 50N 97 10W
7 St. Brieuc, France 48 31N 2 48W
36 St. Christopher
     (St. Kitts), W. I. ...17 20N 62 40W
36 St. Croix, I., W. Indies.17 30N 64 40W
7 St. David's I., Bermuda 35 38N 63 42W
7 St. Denis, France .....48 57N 2 20 E
7 St. Etienne, France ...45 27N 4 22 E
9 St. Gallen, Switz......47 25N 9 22 E
36 St. George, Bermuda .32 24N 64 42W
4 St. George's Channel,
     British Isles.......52 0N 6 0W
10 St. Gotthard Pass,
     Switzerland ....46 33N 8 33 E
25 St. Helena, I.,
     Atlantic Ocean 15 55S 5 44W
4 St. Helens, England ...53 28N 2 43W
33 Saint John, Canada ...45 20N 66 8W
33 St. John's, Canada ...47 33N 52 40W
40 St. Kilda, N.Z. ....45 53S 170 31 E
33 St. Lawrence, Gulf of
     and R., Canada 48 25N 62 0W
33 St. Lawrence, I., Alas..63 0N 170 0W
26 St. Louis, Senegal 16 8N 16 27W
35 St. Louis, U.S.A. 38 40N 90 20W
36 St. Lucia, I.,
     Windward Is. 14 0N 60 50W
7 St Malo, France 48 40N 2 0W
7 St. Maur, France .....48 49N 2 30 E
10 St. Moritz, Switz......46 30N 9 50 E
7 St. Nazaire, France ...47 17N 2 11W
35 St. Paul, U.S.A. 44 54N 93 5W
35 St. Petersburg, U.S.A. .27 45N 82 40W
33 St. Pierre, I., Canada ..46 49N 56 15W
7 St. Quentin, France ...49 55N 3 20 E
7 St. Tropez, France ...43 17N 6 38 E
36 St. Vincent, I.,
     Windward Is.......13 10N 61 10W
7 Saintonge, Prov., Fr. ..45 40N 0 50W
21 Sakai, Japan ....34 35N 135 27 E
21 Sakhalin, I., U.S.S.R...51 0N 143 0 E
8 Salamanca, Spain 40 57N 5 40W
18 Salekhard, U.S.S.R....66 30N 66 25 E
19 Salem, India.........11 39N 78 12 E
35 Salem, U.S.A. 36 5N 80 30W
10 Salerno, Italy ....40 40N 14 44 E
4 Salford, England 53 30N 2 17W
29 Salima, Malawi ......13 47S 34 28 E
4 Salisbury, England ...51 4N 1 48W
29 Salisbury, Rhodesia ..17 50N 31 2 E
34 Salt Lake City, U.S.A..40 45N 112 0W

37 Salta, Argentina 24 48S 65 30W
37 Salto, Uruguay ....31 20S 57 59 E
31 Salvador, Rep.,
     Central America ...13 50N 89 0W
37 Salvador, Brazil 13 0S 38 30W
9 Salzburg, Austria ....47 48N 13 2 E
9 Salzburg, Prov., Aust..47 30N 13 0 E
9 Salzgitter, Germany ..52 12N 10 22 E
17 Samar I., Philippines ..12 0N 125 0 E
17 Samaria, site, Jordan ..32 15N 35 13 E
14 Samarkand, U.S.S.R...39 40N 67 0 E
40 Samoa Is., Pacific Oc. .14 0S 171 0W
11 Samos I., Greece .....37 45N 26 50 E
11 Samothráki I., Greece .40 28N 25 38 E
36 San Andrés I.,
     Caribbean Sea 12 42S 81 46W
37 San Angelo, U.S.A. ...31 30N 100 30W
34 San Antonio, U.S.A. ..29 30N 98 30W
34 San Cristóbal, Ven.... 7 35N 72 24W
34 San Diego, U.S.A. 32 50N 117 10W
36 San Fernando, Trinidad 10 20N 61 30W
34 San Francisco, U.S.A. .37 45N 122 30W
36 San Francisco de Macoris,
     Dominican Rep.....19 19N 70 15W
36 San José, Costa Rica ..10 0N 84 2W
36 San Jose, U.S.A. 37 10N 121 57W
37 San Juan, Argentina ..31 30S 68 30W
36 San Juan, Puerto Rico..18 29N 66 6W
37 San Luis, Argentina ...33 20S 66 20W
36 San Luis Potosi, Mex..22 10N 101 0W
10 San Marino, Rep., It...43 56N 12 25 E
31 San Miguel, Salvador..13 30N 88 12W
37 San Miguel de
     Tucuman, Arg.....26 47S 65 13W
31 San Salvador, Salvador .13 40N 89 20W
36 San Salvador (Watling) I.,
     Bahamas 24 0N 74 40W
8 San Sebastian, Spain ..43 17N 1 58W
18 Sana, Yemen ....15 27N 44 12 E
13 Sandnes, Norway ....58 50N 5 45 E
4 Sandringham, England .52 50N 0 30 E
31 Santa Ana, Salvador ..14 0N 89 40W
34 Santa Barbara Is.,
     U.S.A. 33 40N 119 40W
36 Santa Clara, Cuba 22 20N 80 0W
36 Santa Cruz, Costa Rica.10 15N 85 41W
36 Santa Cruz, Tenerife ..28 29N 16 26W
37 Santa Fé, Argentina ..31 35S 60 41W
37 Santa Maria, Brazil ..29 40S 53 40W
8 Santander, Spain 43 27N 3 51W
8 Santarem, Portugal ...39 12N 8 42W
37 Santiago, Chile 23 24S 70 50W
36 Santiago, Dominican
     Republic 19 30N 70 40W
36 Santiago, Panama 8 0N 81 0W
8 Santiago de Compostela,
     Spain 42 52N 8 37W
36 Santiago de Cuba,
     Cuba 20 0N 75 49W
37 Santiago del Estero,
     Argentina 27 50S 64 20W
36 Santo Domingo,
     Dominican Rep.....18 30N 69 58W
37 Santos, Brazil 24 0S 46 20W
37 São Luis, Brazil 2 39S 44 15W
37 São Paulo, Brazil 23 40S 46 50W
25 São Thomé, I.,
     Gulf of Guinea ..... 0 10N 7 0 E
21 Sapporo, Japan ......43 0N 141 15 E
11 Sarajevo, Yugoslavia ..43 52N 18 26 E
14 Saratov, U.S.S.R. ....51 30N 46 2 E
23 Sarawak, st., Malaysia.. 2 0N 113 0 E
10 Sardinia, I., Italy .....40 0N 9 0 E
5 Sark, I., Br. Isles 49 25N 2 20W
21 Sasebo, Japan ....33 15N 129 50 E
32 Saskatchewan, Prov.,
     Canada 54 40N 106 0W
32 Saskatchewan, R.,
     Canada 53 40N 103 30W
32 Saskatoon, Canada ...52 10N 106 45W
10 Sássari, Sardinia,
     Italy ....40 44N 8 33 E
10 Satu Mare, Rumania ..47 46N 22 55 E
18 Saudi Arabia, st., Asia..26 0N 44 0 E
33 Sault Ste. Marie,
     Canada 46 30N 84 20W
35 Savannah, U.S.A. 32 4N 81 4W
7 Savoie, Prov., France ..45 26N 6 35 E
10 Savona, Italy ....44 19N 8 29 E
22 Sawu, Is., Indonesia ..10 35S 121 50 E
5 Scapa Flow, Orkney,
     Scotland 58 52N 3 0W
4 Scarborough, Eng.....54 17N 0 24W
36 Scarborough, Tobago ..11 11N 60 42W
9 Schleswig-Holstein,
     Land, Germany ....54 10N 9 40 E
9 Schwerin, E. Germany .53 37N 11 22 E
4 Scunthorpe, England ..53 35N 0 38W
34 Seattle, U.S.A. 47 36N 122 20W
8 Segovia, Spain 40 57N 4 10W
7 Seine, R., France .....49 28N 0 15 E
26 Sekondi-Takoradi,
     Ghana 5 2N 1 48W
26 Selibaby, Mauritania ..15 20N 12 15W
5 Selkirk & co., Scot. ...55 33N 2 50W
22 Semarang, Indonesia . 7 0S 110 26 E
14 Semipalatinsk, U.S.S.R.50 30N 80 10 E
21 Sendai, Japan ....31 50N 130 20 E
21 Seoul, S. Korea......37 40N 127 0 E
22 Seremban, Malaysia .. 2 43N 101 53 E
29 Serowe, Botswana ....22 18S 26 58 E
8 Setubal, Portugal 38 30N 8 58W
14 Sevastopol, U.S.S.R...44 35N 33 30 E
4 Severn, R., Wales/Eng..52 15N 2 13W
15 Severnaya Zemlya, Is.,
     U.S.S.R...........79 0N 100 0 E
8 Sevilla, Prov., Spain...37 0N 6 0W
8 Seville, Spain 37 23N 6 0W
31 Seward, Alaska 60 0N 149 30W
4 Seychelles, Is., Ind. Oc..50 0S 56 0 E
26 Sfax, Tunisia ....34 49N 10 40 E
7 's Gravenhage, Neth...52 7N 4 17 E
27 Shahhat, Libya ......32 40N 21 35 E
19 Shahjahanpur, India...27 50N 79 58 E
14 Shakhty, U.S.S.R. ....47 40N 40 10 E
20 Shanghai, China......31 15N 121 30 E
20 Shangkiu, China......34 28N 115 42 E
6 Shannon, R., Ireland ..53 10N 8 0W
6 Shannon Airport,
     Ireland 52 40N 9 0W
20 Shansi, Prov., China ..38 20N 112 0 E
20 Shaohing, China......30 0N 120 32 E

20 Shantung, Prov., China.36 0N 117 30 E
4 Sheerness, England ...51 26N 0 47 E
4 Sheffield, England 53 23N 1 28W
4 Sheppey, I. of, Eng....51 23N 0 50 E
26 Sherbro, I.,
     Sierra Leone 7 30N 12 40W
33 Sherbrooke, Canada ..45 24N 71 57W
5 Shetland Is., Scot. 60 30N 1 30W
34 Sheyenne, R., U.S.A. .47 40N 98 15W
20 Shihkiachwang, China..37 55N 114 30 E
19 Shikarpur, Pakistan ...27 58N 68 42 E
21 Shikoku, I., Japan ....33 30N 133 30 E
21 Shimano, R., Japan ...36 50N 138 30 E
21 Shimizu, Japan ....35 0N 138 30 E
21 Shimonoseki, Japan ...33 58N 131 0 E
18 Shiraz, Iran ....29 42N 52 30 E
21 Shizuoka, Japan ......35 0N 138 30 E
11 Shkodër, Albania .....42 6N 19 29 E
19 Sholapur, India.......17 43N 75 56 E
4 Shrewsbury, Eng.....52 42N 2 45W
4 Shropshire, co., Eng. ..52 36N 2 45W
19 Shwebo, Burma ......22 30N 95 45 E
19 Sialkot, W. Pakistan ..32 32N 74 30 E
22 Siam, G. of, Thailand ..10 0N 102 30 E
20 Sian, China..........34 2N 109 0 E
20 Siangtan, China ......28 0N 112 55 E
10 Sicily, I., Italy ....37 30N 14 0 E
26 Sidi bel Abbes, Alg. ..35 13N 0 45W
4 Sidmouth, England ...50 40N 3 13W
10 Siena, Italy ....43 20N 11 20 E
26 Sierra Leone, st.,
     W. Africa 9 0N 12 0W
8 Sierra Morena, Spain .38 20N 4 0W
8 Sierra Nevada, Spain ..37 3N 3 15W
34 Sierra Nevada, U.S.A..38 0N 120 0W
11 Sighet, Rumania .....47 57N 23 52 E
19 Sikkim, st., N.E. India..27 50N 88 50 E
12 Silkeborg, Denmark ..56 10N 9 32 E
22 Simeulüé, I., Indonesia. 2 45N 95 45 E
14 Simferopol, U.S.S.R...44 55N 34 5 E
19 Simla, India..........31 2N 77 15 E
39 Simpson Desert,
     Australia ....25 0S 137 0 E
17 Sinai Pen., Egypt ....29 0N 34 0 E
27 Singa, Sudan ....13 10N 33 57 E
22 Singapore, st., Asia .. 1 17N 103 51 E
20 Sinhailien, China .....34 35N 119 20 E
20 Sining, China ....36 50N 102 10 E
20 Sinkiang-Uigur
     Autonomous Reg.,
     China ....42 0N 88 0 E
2 Sinop, Turkey ....42 1N 35 11 E
20 Sinsiang, China ......35 30N 113 55 E
20 Sintai, China ....37 1N 114 29 E
21 Sinuiju, N. Korea .....39 59N 124 30 E
5 Sioux City, U.S.A. 42 32N 96 25W
35 Sioux Falls, U.S.A. ...43 35N 96 40W
10 Siracusa, Sicily, Italy ..37 4N 15 17 E
31 Sitka, Alaska 57 5N 135 20W
13 Sjaelland, I., Denmark .55 30N 11 30 E
13 Skagerrak, str.,
     Denmark–Norway ..57 50N 9 0 E
12 Skelleftea, Sweden ...64 45N 20 59 E
13 Skien, Norway ....59 12N 9 35 E
26 Skikda, Algeria ......36 50N 6 49 E
11 Skoplje, Yugoslavia ...42 1N 21 32 E
6 Slaney, R., Ireland ...52 52N 6 45W
6 Sligo & co., Ireland ...54 17N 8 28W
6 Slough, England 51 30N 0 35W
10 Slovenia, Prov.,
     Yugoslavia ....46 10N 14 40 E
4 Smethwick, England ..52 29N 1 58W
4 Smolensk, U.S.S.R....54 45N 32 0 E
12 Snæfell, Mt., Iceland ..64 47N 15 30W
1 Society Is., Pacific Oc..17 0S 151 0W
18 Socotra, I., S. Yemen ..12 30N 54 0 E
13 Söderhamm, Sweden .61 18N 17 10 E
11 Sofia, Bulgaria ......42 45N 23 20 E
26 Sokoto, Nigeria ......13 2N 5 16 E
9 Solingen, Germany ...51 10N 7 4 E
1 Solomon Is., Pac. Oc. . 8 0S 160 0 E
5 Solway Firth, Scot. ...54 40N 3 30W
18 Somali Republic,
     E. Africa .... 5 0N 47 0 E
4 Somerset, co., England.51 9N 3 0W
20 Soochow, China......31 18N 120 41 E
8 Soria, Spain 41 43N 2 32W
29 South Africa, Rep. of .30 0S 25 0 E
1 South America, cont. 12 30 N to 55 30 S
                   35 0W to 81 0W
38 South Australia, st.,
     Australia ....32 0S 139 0 E
35 South Bend, U.S.A. ...41 38N 86 20W
35 South Carolina, st.,
     U.S.A. 33 40N 80 30W
22 South China Sea, Asia..20 0N 115 0 E
34 South Dakota, st.,
     U.S.A. 44 40N 101 0W
40 South Island, N.Z.....44 0S 171 0 E
21 South Korea, Rep. Asia 36 0N 128 0 E
41 South Pole, Ant. 90 0S
5 South Ronaldsay, I.,
     Scotland 58 46N 2 58W
4 South Shields, England.54 59N 1 26W
5 South Uist I., Scotland .57 10N 7 10W
22 South Vietnam, st.,
     Asia ....14 0N 108 40 E
29 South West Africa, st.,
     Africa ....23 0S 17 38 E
18 South Yemen, st., Asia.12 50N 45 0 E
4 Southampton, England.50 54N 1 23W
33 Southampton, I., Can..64 30N 84 0W
4 Southend-on-Sea, Eng.51 32N 0 43 E
40 Southern Alps, N.Z. ..43 41S 170 11 E
1 Southern Ocean 0 0S 160 0W
4 Southport, England ...53 38N 3 1W
15 Sovetskaya Gavan,
     U.S.S.R...........48 50N 140 0 E
41 Sovietskaya, Ant. ....78 7S 78 0 E
8 Spain, st., Europe 40 0N 5 0W
9 Spandau, E. Germany .52 32N 13 13 E
8 Spanish Sahara, Prov.,
     N.W. Africa 25 0N 13 0W
36 Spanish Town, Jamaica 18 0N 77 20W
39 Spencer, G., S. Austral.34 30S 137 0 E
6 Sperrin Mts., N. Ire.....54 50N 7 0W
1 Spitsbergen, Arctic Oc.78 0N 17 0 E
10 Split, Y. Slav.........43 31N 16 28 E
34 Spokane, U.S.A. 47 35N 117 30W
35 Springfield, U.S.A. ...39 48N 89 40W
29 Springs, S. Africa ....26 13S 28 25 E
11 Srbija (Serbia), Prov.,
     Y. Slav............43 30N 21 0 E
15 Sredne Kolymsk,
     U.S.S.R...........67 20N 154 40 E
19 Srinagar, Kashmir,
     India.............34 12N 74 50 E
4 Stafford, England 52 49N 2 9W